Are u ok?

Are u ok?

A Guide to Caring for Your Mental Health

kati morton, LMFT

Da Capo
LIFE
LONG

To my best friend and husband Sean
for always believing in me
even when I didn't believe in myself.
Without your love and encouragement,
nothing is possible.

And to all the kinions out there
who have been with me along the way.
It's because of your courage and support
that I can do what I do.
This book is for you.

contents

contents

author's note

The people and patients I have discussed in this book have charitably given their permission. Many of the stories I share are very personal, and come from those I know in my private life, as well as from my own life experience. To protect the privacy of those mentioned, all names and identifying details have been changed. The stories shared in this book are given to help further illustrate how mental health can affect us. This book is meant to empower you to get the help you need and deserve. It is not a replacement for actual mental health treatment. If you are struggling with mental health issues, I urge you to seek professional help as soon as possible.

prologue

Hey, everyone! My name is Kati Morton, and I am a licensed marriage and family therapist. I started off my career in the mental health field in 2008 with the hope of helping people struggling with mental illness. This career choice just so happened to coincide with a massive shift in the way people were communicating about such things. The conversations about mental health were not happening face to face; instead, they were taking place online.

As a therapist who graduated from Pepperdine University, I could offer a great breadth of knowledge. However, due to the constraints of my license and private practice, I was only able to see people in my local community, meaning my experience and expertise were limited to those who lived in the greater Los Angeles area. This limitation didn't make sense to me. Instead of only being able to give people in specific regions access to necessary mental health knowledge, why not share what I knew with people around the world? So I decided to start a YouTube channel.

I have been creating mental health videos on YouTube for over seven years with the goal of making information more readily available to all. To date, I have made over a thousand videos addressing people's various mental health concerns, and I believe that by talking about mental health in such a public way, the stigma surrounding it can finally cease to exist.

Through my audience, I have become acutely aware of how broken our mental health care systems around the world are. Many in the United Kingdom report having to wait a year to see a therapist, while in the United States we find ourselves battling to get our out-of-pocket costs covered. And these issues don't even touch on the fact that most people are afraid to seek help due to the negative way our media portrays mental illness. I believe my continued engagement in this arena could be a key to significant change, and what ultimately led me to create this book.

As much as we talk about mental health online and in person, we need to learn to crawl before we can run. I hear from people every day asking fundamental questions about their rights in therapy, how to find a good therapist, what type of therapist to look for, etc. It's clear that there is a lack of understanding and communication between mental health professionals and those seeking help. To make sure we are receiving proper care, we need to know what questions to ask, and where to start. That's where *Are u ok?* comes in.

I wrote *Are u ok?* to be your guiding light through the process. By explaining how to know when we need help, and sharing the different types of assistance available, I hope you leave feeling equipped with all the fundamental knowledge necessary to make a positive change in your life. To date, videos on my channel have been viewed over twenty-seven million times, so know that whatever you are feeling or are worried about, you are not alone.

Stigma and fear can only survive when kept secret. By talking more openly and honestly about mental health, we are shining a light on it, proving that it doesn't have to be so scary, and that we all struggle sometimes. So work with me to shed some light on mental health, remind people it's nothing to be ashamed of, and let those around us know there is help available. Hope is such a powerful thing—if we work together, we can ensure this conversation continues and the stigma associated with mental illness disappears for good.

Are u ok?

chapter 1

What Is Mental Health?

What You Should Know and Where to Start

What's the difference between mental health and mental illness? We all have mental health. The term *mental health* is often thought to be synonymous with mental illness, but that is simply not true. Our mental health is how we are doing psychologically and emotionally. In other words, how are you feeling today? And I don't want the thoughtless "I'm fine" answer, but honestly, how are you doing? Are you able to keep up with work or school? How are your relationships? How is your home life? If you're doing pretty well in life, keeping up with your responsibilities, making time for meaningful relationships, and are able to manage any small upset that occurs, I would say your mental health is in good shape.

On the other hand, if you are feeling more tired than usual, not enjoying the things you used to, and a minor upset ruins your entire day, then you may need to put more effort into your mental health. When I am tearful for no reason, I know that I need to take better care of myself. I could cry watching a commercial or get easily upset by a small conflict. Whatever minor issue comes up, I feel so emotionally taxed that I simply can't handle it. When I find myself feeling this way, I know I need to carve out some self-care time as well as call my therapist for a session.

Since we can't see our mental health in the same manner we can often see our physical health, it's an easy thing to ignore. Many people find themselves feeling tearful, easily upset, and emotionally exhausted for years before reaching out to a professional. I constantly hear how people put it off because they think, "It isn't really that bad" or "I can still get up and get to work, so I'm all right." Know that we don't have to wait until we cannot function at all to get help. In fact, our prognosis is better if we get help early on.

Mental illness, on the other hand, occurs when our mental health is compromised or neglected for so long that it affects our ability to function in our everyday life. Meaning that we can't do the things we used to, enjoy what we used to, or even see the world around us as we used to. Mental illness covers a wide range of conditions such as depression, anxiety, eating disorders, and borderline personality disorder. How affected we are by our mental illness depends on how severe our case is, how much support and help we are getting, and how quickly we sought out help.

> Mental illness occurs when our mental health is compromised or neglected for so long that it affects our ability to function in our everyday life.

Mental illness can feel like our mind is actually fighting against us, keeping us from the

2

things we love, and making everyday tasks much harder. Just as we would talk about a cold or flu in our body, our brain is sick and needs professional attention. That's why I constantly remind people to think of mental illness just as they would a physical illness. Would you tell someone who had pneumonia to get up and finish their workday? Or would we expect someone with a broken leg to go about their day in the same way they did before the break? Of course not! So why is it that we often don't take mental illnesses as seriously as we do physical ones?

I had a patient many years ago who suffered from flu-like symptoms for months. She felt achy, tired, and nauseous and would vomit sometimes. Her husband took her to doctors, specialists, and even a neurologist to figure out what was going on. They found nothing. All her blood tests and scans came back normal. My patient was upset, felt lost, hopeless, and her husband started to wonder if she was making it all up. So they came to see me.

I vividly remember my patient's husband asking me, "Kati, do you think it's just all in her head?" I struggled with how to manage an answer to this while being respectful of both him and his wife, but what I really wanted to blurt out was "Why would that matter?" If her problems were psychosomatic (meaning her physical symptoms were caused by mental illness), did that make her symptoms less important? Doesn't our brain run everything in our body and ensure that we can do all we need to do each day? If we have that understanding, why do we still struggle to take our mental health as seriously as we do our physical health?

I did end up saying something like "Well, in truth I don't think the origin matters. What is important is how we are going to get her feeling better." In the end, it turned out that her intense anxiety and bouts of depression were making her ill. Once she started taking an antidepressant and learned some helpful behavioral techniques, the symptoms went away—but I don't really see how that's different from her actually having the flu. Either way, she was sick and needed professional help to feel better, right?

Just How Common Are Mental Illnesses?

If you worry that having a mental illness is odd or a rarity, just consider that worldwide one person in five is affected by mental illness.[1] What that means to me is that everyone has been impacted in some way, whether we know someone close to us who struggles with mental illness, or we have experienced it ourselves. I would even argue that the number can't be entirely representative because so many people are suffering in silence, too scared to get the help they desperately need.

It's also important to know that a mental illness isn't always something that follows us for our entire lives. If we get the proper help and follow through with what our treatment team (meaning our therapist, psychiatrist, doctor, etc.) says, we can limit the amount of time we are affected by our mental illness. I compare having a mental illness to my body's propensity for strep throat. I used to get it at least three times each winter, and even though I got my tonsils removed at the ripe age of twenty-three, it still comes back from time to time.

Now I have a plan to stop it before it starts, and know what to do if I feel it coming on. First, I start drinking tea with honey and take oregano oil and vitamin C each morning. If I start to feel soreness in my throat, I call my doctor and get in to see him immediately. He runs the tests quickly and either gives me an oral antibiotic, or if it's bad, I get a steroid shot. Either way, it only lasts for a week at most. The same goes for our mental health.

There are things we are going to have to do each and every day to keep our illness at bay, but if it starts getting worse we will need to see a professional. The more we practice these preventative measures, the less likely it will be that we will continue to need professional help.

Anxiety is the most common mental illness in the United States, affecting more than forty million adults (that's roughly 18 percent of the population).[2] Anxiety is something we naturally feel when we are in a scary, dangerous, or unfamiliar situation. It is what keeps us safe and tells us when something is off, just like our fight-or-flight response. It only becomes a problem when the level of anxiety we feel is irrational or disproportionate to the situation, meaning that we may feel extreme anxiety about being outside of our home, or meeting new people. It can stop us from eating, sleeping, and concentrating. Anxiety symptoms can vary from person to person, even expressing themselves physically like they do for Alice:

> First, I start breathing harder and get panicky, and then I feel angry, and I just lie on my bed wanting to cry or scream. I'm also very irritable recently, yet I know I shouldn't yell at anyone, so I bottle it all up inside. Is this all part of my anxiety?

The truth is, yes, all those symptoms can be part of our anxiety, but since many of these symptoms mimic those of a physical illness, people with anxiety are three to five times more likely to wind up at their doctor's office or hospital.[3] I only mention this so you can be open to the idea that what you physically feel may come from something going on psychologically. I am not saying it's all in your head and you are not in need of care or understanding; but rather that no matter where it comes from, you feel that way, it's warranted, and knowing its origin can help us find you the proper care.

Lastly, remember that anxiety is not stress. Many people misunderstand and think that when we are stressed out because of a big presentation or test that what we are experiencing is anxiety, but that couldn't be more wrong. Stress has a trigger, a reason for its existence in your life, while anxiety doesn't. Many of my patients with anxiety didn't even know that what they were feeling was anxiety until their doctors referred them to me. More often than not, they don't know what triggers it. It can feel like it comes out of nowhere, bothers them for a long time, and no matter what they try to do it won't go away.

While depression is less common than anxiety, affecting 15.7 million adults in the United States, the thing to consider as we briefly talk about depression is that 3 to 5 percent of adults will suffer from a depressive episode in their lifetime.[4] I honestly think the number is much higher, but if we don't reach out for help, how can anyone know we are suffering? Also, something to remember about depression (as well as other mental illnesses) is that it's *episodic*, meaning it comes and goes. We can have episodes of depression that last for a few weeks up to months, and then they go away like they were never there. I believe it's because of these episodes that people don't reach out for help. All of those terrible "I can't get out of bed" feelings go away and we think maybe we were making it all up, or it's really not that bad and we can work through it on our own. Then they come back, and we go through the same cycle all over again, possibly not getting help for years.

I blame myself and people like me for why depression so often goes undiagnosed and treated. I think it's because our teachers drill lists of symptoms into our heads about what depression is supposed to look and feel like to those who suffer from it. The truth is that depression doesn't always show itself in the way we expect. It can be quiet, sneaky, and shift over time. Some of the most common symptoms I have seen, which are not listed on any diagnostic criteria, are:

- Feeling like you are walking through water: everything is harder, and you feel like you're moving so much slower.

- Reading and rereading the same thing. Concentration is very hard to come by.

- Everyone around you is just so freaking irritating!

- You can't help but replay everything you have ever done wrong in your life.

I know these symptoms may seem too vague or as if they can be applied to many illnesses, but it's important to highlight just how varied depression can feel. It's not always about feeling sad or struggling to sleep; it can look and feel very different person to person. Just remember that however you feel, if you don't feel like yourself and find that you are less and less interested in things you used to like, please get help.

The lack of energy that comes along with depression is always my largest concern. Many people who come into my office or reach out online tell me they just couldn't muster up the energy to reach out any sooner. Or if they did try to reach out, their therapist or doctor didn't call them back and they gave up. When simply showering and getting out of bed become huge successes, then calling and making an appointment for therapy, checking your insurance to make sure it's covered, getting to the office on time, and expressing what you are feeling is just not feasible.

That's why depression can hold people hostage for so long. When we have the energy to get up and out of the house, we don't think we feel bad enough to need any help or treatment.

By the time we actually do feel bad enough and believe we need to get some help, we physically and mentally can't. This is why we need not only to do our best to check in on our own mental health, but also to have supportive people in our lives who can help us when we can't help ourselves. This could be having that friend make the call to see a therapist, or driving us to our appointment and waiting with us. However we can make it happen, it's important that we have a plan to get back up and keep fighting.

Many years ago, I was at a women's convention and heard one of the most motivational speeches of my life. There was much to digest in this speech, but my key takeaway was this question:

Why in real life when we trip and fall do we get back up
so quickly, yet when we emotionally fall down, we allow
ourselves to lie on the ground for weeks, possibly years?

The reason I like this question so much is that it's brutally accurate. If I trip and fall in real life, I bounce back up, look around (hope nobody saw), brush myself off, and go on my way. Emotionally, on the other hand, I can replay a bad or hurtful thing that happened over and over, essentially holding myself pinned to the ground where the incident took place. It baffles me why I do this, and I am still working to more quickly process hurts and changes so I can get up, dust myself off, and move on.

Take some time to consider this. Would you allow yourself to trip and fall only to lie on the sidewalk while others walked past? Of course not! Then why when we trip up emotionally do we allow that to happen? For many it's because it's embarrassing to admit and harder to face than just pretending it never happened. Others share how they didn't even realize they were on the ground in the first place! Whatever the reason, I think this question is something we should all consider. Especially as we talk about the stigma associated with mental illness and how we all play a role in fostering it.

Why Is Mental Illness So Stigmatized?

We all add to the stigma surrounding mental illness. I am not trying to call anyone out or make anyone feel bad, but in our own way we each contribute to the stigma. It could be the way we think about other people with mental illness, or even the way we talk to ourselves about our own struggles. As an example, we could (without realizing it) assume that all people with schizophrenia live on the streets and talk to themselves, or that every depressed person should just get up and shower; that will make them feel so much better. I know these are varied examples, but whether we like to admit it or not, we all have biases and live our lives based on our beliefs and experiences. We should all take some time to think about the mental illnesses we know of and what our thoughts or beliefs are about them. Be honest, because we have to truly recognize our own prejudices before we can work to change them.

Some of our assumptions or prejudices about mental illness can actually be helpful; when confronted with a mentally ill person they may make us more patient or encourage us to communicate more clearly, so there isn't a misunderstanding. Other assumptions can be hurtful and isolate us. I believe the best way to manage our thoughts is to first educate ourselves. We need to fully understand how a mental illness can feel to someone before we can thoughtfully talk about it. Second, for a moment, try to put yourself in their position. How would that affect you and your life? Could you do all you do each day with that illness? I find this to be the part where people who may have judged others prematurely have that ah-ha! moment. It can be powerful to consider what you could and couldn't do as a result of your mental health. Consider this concept as we move through the next two mental illnesses.

I saved these for last because they are by far the most stigmatized and misunderstood, each for very different reasons. But let's start by talking about eating disorders (EDs), since they are my specialty. EDs are an interesting mix of physical and mental health, and why I have always believed the two are inextricably linked, whether we want to admit it or not ("healthy mind, healthy body" is my motto for a reason). When we overeat, starve ourselves, binge and purge, exercise too much, or whatever our eating disorder tells us to do, we are affecting our physical health because of our mental illness. It is because our mind and body are so linked with this illness that eating disorders have the highest mortality rate of any mental illness.

The biggest misunderstanding about eating disorders is that they are all about the food. In truth, they have nothing to do with food. It's all about why we decided that controlling our food intake was necessary and what we get out of doing so. Do we do it because if we eat until we are uncomfortably full, we can't possibly think about anything else? Do we feel so sick and sad inside that we want our outsides to mirror those feelings? The reasons people have eating disorders are endless and very personal to those who struggle.

Another misconception is that eating disorders only cause people to be underweight. I know that's what the media emphasizes and what we see on most shows or movies about EDs, but the truth is that eating disorders come in all shapes and sizes. I vividly remember walking through the parking lot of a Walgreens and seeing a van rocking back and forth. I figured kids were in there messing around, or possibly adults, but what I saw forever changed the way I view eating disorders.

The woman in the van had just come through a Carl's Jr. drive-through and was moving around quickly to get all her food set out on the dashboard. Her fast movements were causing the van to rock as she hastily ate through her stack of binge food. I know this image isn't as shocking as the underweight version we are used to, but it's just as serious and dangerous, and the stigma even more intense. There was a reason she was doing this at night in a pretty empty parking lot, alone. Many who suffer from binge eating disorder (BED) do so in silence, never reaching out for help, wondering why they can't stop eating after they are full.

When you combine the stigma people attach to EDs with society's judgment of those who are overweight, it's no wonder most sufferers don't reach out for help. I have worked at many eating disorder treatment centers over the years, yet never treated someone with BED. This isn't because the treatment centers wouldn't take them, but because insurance companies wouldn't pay for their care. If they were not underweight, companies would deny our plea for coverage, and unless the patient could afford the $35,000 cost, or more, each month, they wouldn't be admitted to the program. The way our society views what "sick enough" looks like makes the illnesses themselves so much more severe and shame filled.

I don't say all this to deter anyone from getting help or to make you feel bad for those who are struggling. I only say this to make you aware and start a conversation. I find that by simply talking about the things I find upsetting, and shedding light on something that often goes unnoticed, we can enact change. Eating disorders (like all mental illnesses) thrive in the dark, in the shame and embarrassment. So let's shed a little light, offer a little understanding, and (fingers crossed) spark some hope.

The final mental illness I want to discuss is borderline personality disorder (BPD), which I believe is possibly the most stigmatized and misunderstood mental illness out there. If you don't know what BPD is, it is a personality disorder marked by fear of abandonment, emotion disregulation, and difficulty in relationships. The best phrase I have ever heard to describe BPD is "they are emotional burn victims." Meaning that those with BPD feel everything so intensely and painfully that it makes it hard for them to manage any emotion.

What pains me most about BPD is not just that the illness is usually misunderstood, but that it's often born out of abuse. Many who have BPD will share stories of emotional neglect and physical or sexual abuse. Not having any real way to cope, they turn inward and tell themselves terrible and hurtful things. Over time they believe these things to be fact and act out of that supposition. Many of these "facts" are things like "I deserve to be alone, and always will be," "I am not worthy of real love," and "everyone will always end up leaving me." It is because of these false beliefs that those with BPD lash out at others; it's not because they are mean. They just hurt so much all the time.

The stigma associated with BPD doesn't only occur in normal everyday life; it also exists within the mental health community. Many therapists, counselors, and psychiatrists will not treat patients with borderline personality disorder, stating that they are too difficult and require more time than an outpatient (meaning you see them once a week or so and then go about your life) professional can offer. I find this to be the most harmful kind of stigma. This means that when we are struggling and we reach out, we may be referred to someone else and seen for a bit, only to be told we need different or more extensive care; we may be passed around from therapist to therapist only to be left without any care at all.

I fully believe the reason many professionals won't treat someone with BPD is that they don't fully understand it. If we can work together to increase knowledge of BPD, where it comes from, and what treatments work best, then I really think we can start offering real help to those who need it.

chapter 2

Why Can It Feel So Hard to Get Better?

Whether or not you have a mental illness, we all struggle with mental health from time to time. But good news: there is so much we can do to make you feel better! Often, by learning some simple techniques to modify how we think and act in certain situations, we can stop things from getting any worse. Our brain is so adaptive, and it enjoys routines; but although that is usually a good thing (e.g., learning new job tasks, getting ready easily in the morning), it can also keep us stuck in a rut of unhealthy behaviors that impair our ability to function.

That rut is why when life gets extra stressful or upsetting our mind wants to go back to an unhealthy action. If you think about it, it is an easier thing to do: we have done it a million times and we don't have to think about it. When we are learning new, healthier behaviors, we really have to fight to keep out of that old rut. That's why you will hear me continually stress that getting help sooner rather than later is preferable. If we don't create such a deep rut, we won't have to fight too hard to keep out of it. Also, we can more quickly develop a healthy rut that runs deeper than the unhealthy one.

When we are born, our brain works overtime learning how to get our needs met. We cry, we learn muscle control and movement, and we begin to get a feeling for our world. Since we are talking about learning unhealthy and healthy behaviors, let's talk about nurture for a moment (even though nature plays a role as well), and how those around us can affect our mental health.

When, as infants, we cry, someone is supposed to come and help us; it's our only way of letting anyone know we are in need. When we are fed and suck and swallow, our brains and nervous systems are wired to calm down and be soothed. If when, as babies, we cry and no one comes to get us, soothe us, and take care of us, we may decide to stop crying. Why waste the energy? Or if when we cry we are punished and still not given the help we need, we will slowly learn that how we feel and what we think we need aren't right. We may even start to believe that we can only count on ourselves for care, and no one else. This can lead to us thinking that our feelings aren't important to anyone else, and if we need something done we have to do it ourselves.

I know this may seem like an intense example, but I want you to understand why we act the way we do. Why do we have such a hard time trusting ourselves, how we feel, and knowing what we want? Sometimes the answers can go as far back as to when we were infants and spoke up about our needs, only to be told we were wrong or not deserving. It can make us question everything we think and feel. When we feel a particular emotion or desire, we can't just act on it and know it will be okay. Instead, we may stuff it inside and tell ourselves we don't really know what we want or need. Sometimes we may need someone else to tell us it's okay and validate what we want and need.

I know claiming that some things go back to our infancy seems like an outdated idea, but whether we recognize it or not, we have all been told at one time or another that how we felt wasn't okay. While we don't have any control over that, we do have the ability to accept or not accept the message. We can decide that we are worth it, that how we feel is important and valid, and that we deserve to be loved and cared for. These positive and self-affirming decisions we can make are really at the root of what I do in my therapy practice, and why therapy can be so life changing.

> While we can't simply undo all of the emotional upset we may have sustained during our life, we can work to change how we respond to life moving forward.

Getting Out of These Thought Cycles

While we can't simply undo all of the emotional upset we may have sustained during our life, we can work to change how we respond to life moving forward. We can also work to better understand which negativities we are still holding on to and acting out of. I like to use the phrase "acting out of" because it's as though we have been given a role in a play and we have to stick to our character's description. But just as in the theater, we don't have to accept the role. We can say no, or pick another character—one that's more fitting.

Nothing can get done without first understanding ourselves and where we are at. That's why I like to always start by having patients write out who they think their character is: where they came from, what they have been through, and how they present to others. Taking some time to figure out where we came from can help us better navigate where we want to go.

I find that we often get stuck in unhealthy patterns because we don't really know they are unhealthy, or even realize we are doing anything bad for us. Since, possibly, we have been acting and thinking like this for much of our lives, it can be hard to consider that those behaviors are wrong or bad. These thoughts and actions may have even saved your life when you were young. I am constantly reminding my patients that their eating disorders or addictions actually helped them survive during their upbringing, and they should be thankful for that. But they must also remember that those coping skills are no longer serving them and are now only hurting their growth.

What I mean by this is that we may have grown up in a very volatile family where things felt completely out of control. Let's say our dad was an alcoholic; he was erratic and could get physically abusive if we didn't do everything just as he said. To have something under our control we could count on and focus on (because no one wants to focus on abuse or upset), we focused on food and our body. This could mean we numbed out by getting overly full so we couldn't think of anything else, or we didn't eat so all we could think about was how hungry we were.

I know this is hard to fully grasp, but many mental illnesses are only coping skills for other things going on in our life. Like I said earlier, we are adaptive, and to survive through an incredibly difficult time we may have had to distract or numb out with unhealthy activities. Luckily for us, we can completely change the way we adapt and cope! It just takes a little bit of self-reflection and a lot of practice. Don't expect these changes to happen quickly.

We start by first understanding what our character description is, otherwise known as where we are now. I know this can be hard to start, but maybe some of these questions will get you moving in the right direction.

- Are you a leading actor in your family play or do you have a supporting role?

- Do you have a lot of speaking parts? Why or why not?

- What do you do first when you are really upset and feel out of control?

- When you were growing up, was it okay to be mad or sad? How did your parents respond?

- If something was going on in your home, did you feel free to talk about it?

- Are there things about you those closest to you say they love? What about things they don't like?

After answering these questions, we can work to get to where we want to be. The second step is understanding how we talk to ourselves. Yes, I know you talk to yourself and, no, that doesn't make you crazy. We all do it whether we realize it or not. It's how we move through our day, decide what we want to eat, or how we want to navigate a difficult decision or argument. So take some time to notice what you say most to yourself about yourself. Are these loving and confident thoughts or negative and self-deprecating ones? In all honesty, everyone I have do this exercise is surprised at how terribly they talk to themselves, so no extra judgment is needed here.

Once we recognize that nasty, negative stuff we have been saying over and over, let's work to talk back. You know, argue back as if someone in real life said those things to your face! How would you respond to that sort of hate? You may have to argue back using someone else's voice because using your own is too hard. That's fine. It can often help to do this in the voice of that tough friend who doesn't take shit from anyone. Whatever you have to do, fight back! Only then can you change your thoughts and, in turn, your life. I know that sounds really simple, but it honestly is. We don't have to stay who we are.

> We don't have to stay who we are.

Did you know that there are animals that can change their color and shape to stave off predators? It's true! They can do it to blend in and not be detected, or to appear much larger than they are. I love this fact because it's a great reminder that we aren't stuck being who we are now. We can decide we want to change, and with some hard work we can become an entirely different version of ourselves. Freeing, isn't it?

I personally like the visual of being a snake shedding its skin, since it does it often, and as needed. I believe we too need to drop past versions of ourselves often, and as needed, so we aren't holding on to things that no longer serve our purpose. Many of my patients have found this exercise to be empowering: they imagine seeing a person from their past on the street and feel confident the person wouldn't recognize them. Here is one of my favorite quotes from Joan Didion about this concept:

> I have already lost touch with a couple of people I used to be.

So remember that you can always change. There is no age limit or statute of limitation. Each day is a new opportunity to become the person we know at our core we are.

Why Being Uncomfortable Is a Good Thing

Insanity is doing the same thing over and over and expecting a different result. Therefore, if we want to turn our life around, be a better friend, parent, husband, wife, etc., we need to try something different. I warn you, it will be uncomfortable at first because it's new and scary. Something I remember my therapist telling me when I had just finished processing a bad breakup (and even worse relationship) and decided I was ready to date again was "Kati, I really want you to be uncomfortable in your next relationship." At first I was offended; was she telling me she didn't want me to fall in love or be happy? How dare she say something so hurtful!

She explained that wasn't what she meant at all. She was actually wishing me the best and hoping I wouldn't have another terrible and chaotic relationship: that I could get out of my old pattern and find someone who would be caring, thoughtful, and make time for me. Since I hadn't had any of that for years, contemplating getting those things in a relationship could possibly be uncomfortable for me. And it was. But I sat with it, and slowly it wasn't so uncomfortable.

We wouldn't start a new class or job without the understanding that it was going to be hard at first, each task taking more time than it should, not knowing anyone, and feeling a bit awkward. So keep that in mind while you make these small changes, because you are starting something entirely new. It can be frustrating and slow at first, but just like anything new, it will get easier and easier as we keep at it. Each time we talk back to those negative thoughts, we will find them coming back less and less. Slowly but surely we can rewrite our character description, and become who we want to be.

Why Our Brain Is Built for Change

Our brain can get comfortable with what we do each day. Changing that routine or pattern can feel a bit off at first, but it can get comfortable with a new way of doing things too. We can use this to our advantage and know that each time we fight that urge to do things the old way, the healthy rut gets deeper and deeper, making it harder for us to fall back into old habits. I have always loved how flexible our brain can be because it means that no matter how old we are or how long we have been doing things one way, we can learn new things and change. (Yes, you can in fact teach an old dog new tricks!) It all starts with a small change in how we talk to ourselves, and what we decide we want to listen to.

Whatever it may be, we are working to recover from it and move forward. Keep that motto in mind—"It's a process, not perfection"— as you start taking these first steps.

Much of what we hear about mental health and mental illness is negative. Whether the media is using it as an explanation for a crime or there is talk of another celebrity suicide, the focus always tends to lean in a negative direction, creating the belief that those who have a mental illness should be feared or locked up. What I hope this chapter has done for you is open your eyes to what constitutes mental health versus mental illness, remind you that you are not alone, and let you know there is hope.

Let's get started today! Too often I hear people say they waited years to finally reach out or make the changes they so desperately needed, and looking back wish they had decided to do those things earlier. Now is your chance. Is there something that has been bothering you for a while? Forgiveness that you haven't been able to give to yourself or someone in your life? Even though the changes we have talked about so far may seem insignificant, focused on conversations we have within ourselves, they have the ability to affect our entire lives. When we start to feel better about ourselves, we can't help but spread that around.

One of the mottos on my channel is "It's a process, not perfection." It means that our recovery path won't be easy and direct, but we will get there if we keep trying. I have always used *recovery* as an all-encompassing term because we are all in recovery from something. It could be that we lost a loved one or just got out of a depressive episode; whatever it may be, we are working to recover from it and move forward. Keep that motto in mind as you start taking these first steps.

There's no room for judgment on this path, only compassion and understanding. We all slip up, fall back into old patterns, and want to quit. That doesn't mean you don't deserve to get better and have the life you want, or that you aren't worth the fight. It just means that you are human, you are learning something new, and life is really hard sometimes. That's why I try and keep any and all strategies I offer my patients small and easily achievable. We need to have things we can quickly turn to when things get harder; they can remind us of how capable we are.

So be nice to yourself as you start this journey; be patient, and know that if you keep trying, you will only get closer to the person you want to be. When you find your mind going back to negative thoughts, notice the shift, and pull your mind back to the great things about you and all that you are. If it helps, keep a list of the top five things you love about yourself and your life. Pull it out when times get tough so you have a constant reminder of why you are working on this in the first place: to live a life filled with only things like those on your list, and nothing more.

Top Five Things
I Love About Myself and My Life

1. I love my work. It allows me to reach people all over the world.

2. My husband, Sean. He is my consistent comfort.

3. I am thankful for my determination. It allows me to finish what I need to finish.

4. I love where I live. Southern California has beautiful weather and amazing outdoor activities!

5. My body. It allows me to do what I need to each day.

Key Takeaways

- Our brain is adaptive, which is great because that means we can change! It also means it can get used to bad or unhealthy habits easily, and that's why we must make conscious decisions to act in healthy ways.

- Notice what you say to yourself each and every day. It's all those mean things we repeat day after day that cause us to feel inadequate, or push us back into unhealthy habits.

- Once we know what we are saying, we have to talk back! Imagine that those nasty phrases are being said about someone you love, and argue back with a positive statement. By turning all those negatives into positives, we can improve how we feel every day.

- Change can be good, but it can also be scary and uncomfortable. Know that's okay and perfectly normal. If we push through the discomfort we are feeling, we can finally get to that happier and healthier place we have been dreaming of.

- Be gentle with yourself as you take these first few steps. Changing the way we talk to and think about ourselves takes time and practice. That's why I always remind my patients and viewers that it's a process, not perfection.

chapter 3

How Do I Know If I Need Help?

Warning Signs and What to Look For

We all find ourselves running on empty. Maybe we didn't sleep well, eat properly, or feel free from stress in over a month. Whatever it may be, our society focuses more on success and perception than it does on actual health. Many wonder what "not doing well" really means, or how sick one has to be to reach out. Since mental health is something that can't be seen on a scan or X-ray, we argue with ourselves over what defines "sick enough," and even consider that we could be making it all up. One in six adults is affected by a mental illness, yet only about 50 percent actually see a mental health professional for treatment.[1] I believe this is the state of our world because no one talks about it; the only conversations being had are those in our own heads. Let's change that by having a real discussion about mental illness and getting help for it.

I defined the difference between mental health and mental illness; now let's take it a step further and describe what necessitates actual treatment. I advocate seeking therapy whenever you are struggling to work through an issue. This could be as simple as a fight with a parent or spouse, or as complicated as trying to overcome past abuse. If your ability to do what you want and need is hindered by something, see someone about it! Just as a splinter can fester if not pulled out, so can an emotional issue if it's not talked through. In other words, don't wait until it's a mental illness; take that first step and take care of your mental health quickly.

What to consider when seeking help really depends on you and how much you are able to do when you are feeling good versus feeling bad. It's not vital that you meet a certain number of criteria, or that you have been struggling for a specific amount of time; it's more about what you want and hope to do compared to what you feel able to do.

Needing Help versus Having a Diagnosis

I want to differentiate between needing help and being diagnosed. When I use the term *diagnose* I am referring to whether or not we meet the criteria for a mental illness as it is listed in the *Diagnostic and Statistical Manual of Mental Disorders (DSM)*. We can be having a hard time and want to talk it out with someone, but that doesn't mean we have a diagnosable mental illness. I do not believe we need to fit into some measurable list to get help from a professional. Here's an example:

I have been feeling off lately. I am not sure what it is, but I know that I can't sleep, I am crying at work, and I feel

so tired all the time. I went to see my doctor, and he told
me that it was probably stress, but this happens every
few months for about a week! I have a big presentation
at work next week, and I can't keep dealing with this! If
I tried to see a therapist, would they be able to help me?
Or would I just be wasting their time?

If I were to only consider the diagnostic criteria, I would not
be able to tell this person that what they are experiencing is major depressive disorder (MDD). Even though many of her symptoms are similar to those of someone with MDD, she hasn't been
struggling with these feelings for at least two weeks, which is
what the diagnosis requires. She also doesn't talk about changes
in appetite but does say she hasn't been sleeping. Based on the
information we have, this is a mental health issue that has not yet
become a diagnosable mental illness.

It is important to highlight the difference between diagnosis
and the need for treatment because the common misconception
is that we have to wait until we are entirely debilitated to receive
help. This distorted way of thinking is supported by health insurance companies that only care about money, as well as professionals who suck at their jobs and misdiagnose and mistreat
those who seek their help.

I finally decided that I needed to see someone about my
feelings of anxiety and panic. At my first appointment
with a psychiatrist, he told me that I was just overthinking
it and gave me some breathing exercises to do. I tried to
tell him I had used those before and they didn't help, but
he was already leaving. I have never felt worse, or more
like a fool. I guess I was making it all up and I shouldn't
have even bothered.

Unfortunately, examples like the one above are typical and can prevent us from getting the help we so desperately need and deserve. I always tell my patients and viewers that no one knows how you feel better than you do. Sure, you may be doing just fine at work or school. You may even be able to keep up with most of what is asked of you, but you know you don't feel like yourself. If that means you have to argue with your insurance company, or try out four or five different therapists, stick with it. Trust me, all the energy you are putting in now will pay off in the end. Trust how you feel, and what you know about your mood and abilities, and push for the treatment you need to get back to your usual self.

Bottom line: we cannot limit treatment to those who meet the criteria of a mental illness. If we do, we are forcing people to wait until they are ill to have the option to get better. What that does is tell those who are struggling that they aren't sick enough or haven't suffered long enough. If someone went to a doctor's office with a hairline fracture of the leg, they wouldn't be told to return when the leg was actually broken, right? Mental health treatment should be no different.

If We Don't Need a Diagnosis, What Does "Sick Enough" Look Like?

About five years ago I had one of the hardest years of my life. I was planning my wedding, I was studying to take my licensing exam, and working three jobs. I remember walking into a weekly staff meeting and my good friend Johanna whispering, "Are you okay? You don't look like yourself." I wasn't. I wasn't sleeping well, I was working long hours during the week, and taking my

licensing exam prep classes on the weekends, all the while trying to plan my wedding. With even just the mention that I didn't
look like myself, I began to cry. Not because I was sad or upset
about anything in particular, but because I was maxed out. I
was on the verge of tears constantly, even tearing up just from
listening to a sad song on the radio. I also found myself snapping
at anyone who gave me any pushback. I didn't feel like myself;
not at all.

Even though that year was extremely trying and exhausting, I
still didn't technically meet the criteria for a mental illness, but I
knew I needed help. I had been in and out of therapy since I was
a teenager, so I was well aware of what was okay and not okay
for me. Crying at a staff meeting was probably not a good sign,
and I knew I would need to get back in to see my therapist as
soon as possible. I don't expect this story to describe how you
will feel when you know you need to see a therapist; however,
I hope that by walking you through my experience you can find
bits and pieces that resonate with you.

For me to know when I need some outside support, I first
have to know what's normal for me. I know that I usually need
eight or nine hours of sleep to function, I am hungry every four
hours, and I am overall pretty patient and able to multitask with
ease throughout my varied schedule. Keeping all of that in mind,
if one or more of those things is off, I know I am headed for di-
saster. Even as I write this, I remember that before crying at work
(when I finally acknowledged that I needed help), I wasn't eating
lunch until much later in the day because I was so busy I would
forget. I also had been waking up earlier than usual and wasn't
able to fall back asleep. Both of those changes were signs that I
wasn't functioning at my best, and if I had taken notice earlier, I
could have saved myself a lot of frustration and embarrassment.

What Constitutes Needing Help, Then?

We all have varying levels of functioning. What that means is we all have differing amounts of things we can accomplish every day. I am not going to be able to do everything a surgeon does. For starters, I don't have the same education level, and I also know that I cannot focus on one thing for more than forty-five minutes without needing a break. They do ten-plus-hour surgeries and work twelve or more hours each day. I just could not keep up. I cannot function at that level.

That's why the first thing I want you to do is to think about all you can do when you are having a good day. How much can you do when you have slept well, eaten well, and are feeling pretty good? What's your inner dialogue like? Are you kind, more patient, maybe even more loving to those around you? Perhaps you are able to be more productive at work and at home. If you haven't had a day like that in a while, it could help to think back to the last time you felt accomplished, really laughed, or experienced genuine connection with someone. These good days are examples of what "fully functioning" looks and feels like for you.

Then I want you to notice how much you can do when you feel bad. Let's say you've had a fight with someone you love and you haven't had an appetite or been able to sleep through the night, or maybe you are having some health issues. Whatever it is, notice how this differs from your good days. Are you able to compare the two? Maybe when you aren't at your best you are short-tempered, always tired, or unable to concentrate. Knowing both of these extremes helps us better understand our overall functionality in daily life.

Having all this information and understanding about yourself can help you know when something is off. Sometimes keeping notes can help us see if there's a time of the year or even month when we struggle the most. I would notice not only the lows but also the highs, as any deviation from our usual levels means something is going on. For example, when it comes to diagnosing depression, therapists are trained to ask if there have been any changes in sleep or appetite. This could be an increase or decrease in either of those things, as either change counts as a symptom of major depressive disorder.

If you start to feel that you aren't quite yourself, you aren't responding to those you care about in your normal way, and there's been a shift in your ability to do what you usually do in a day, speak to someone. We don't have to be at rock bottom, unable to leave our bed or shower, to talk to a mental health professional. We just have to not feel like ourselves.

What If I Don't Know What a Good or Bad Day Looks Like?

You may be shocked to learn that many adults do not know how to properly identify their feelings. When asked how their week has been or how they are feeling at the moment, many respond with "Eh, just kind of blah" or "I don't know, it's just been a lot. I don't even know where to start." Not knowing how you have really been feeling or what constitutes a good versus a lousy day is very normal. They don't teach us in school how to pinpoint what we are feeling or how to express it; that's something that's supposed to be taught at home. But let's be honest: most parents aren't sitting us down to tell us how to adequately express what we feel.

This lack of emotional education continues into adulthood, when we are expected to pull it together, get over it, and be responsible without anyone openly telling us that what we feel is okay. The truth is that acting like an adult isn't something we will be able to do unless we can correctly process all that we think each day. I know this already sounds overwhelming, but I promise you: I will make it very simple.

Let's start with identifying our emotions. At the end of each day, take some time to write down three to five emotions you felt. They don't have to make sense or go in any particular order; in fact, you can feel angry and then excited within moments. So leave your personal judgment at the door and take some time to dive into yourself. How do you feel now? What happened during your day today, and how do you think about it? Write some feelings down and start keeping track of them. When we don't take the time to notice what we are feeling in the moment, we can push it to the back of our minds only to have something trivial bring it all flooding back. By taking the time to identify our emotions as we experience them, we are giving ourselves the opportunity to better manage them.

The next step in emotional awareness is to describe the emotion beyond the word used to identify it. Meaning that if the emotion we are feeling is anger, what does anger feel like? How does it present itself in your body, relationships, and overall experience? For me, I would say that anger feels like an impulsive fire that jumps to conclusions and bursts out without warning. It feels out of control, downright terrifying, and in all honesty, I avoid it as much as possible. Take a moment and consider what anger (or whatever emotion you would like to start with) feels like to you. Be as vivid as you can, and try to use all your senses. Go through each emotion you felt today and describe it.

Knowing how emotion is experienced in our body, mind, and relationships helps us better understand ourselves. Not just how we interact with others, but how we experience life. If we are not enjoying our life, or it doesn't seem to take much to completely throw us off, now would be an excellent time to seek help. Having all this insight into our inner being and what we feel each day will aide in our therapy and move it along more quickly. That's why taking the time to listen to what our body and mind are already telling us is the best first step.

Feelings are much like waves, we can't stop them from coming, but we can choose which one to surf.
—*Jonatan Mårtensson*

Why Therapy Can Be Helpful to Anyone

I know I just finished telling you all the ways we can understand that we need to start seeing someone for our mental health, but in all honesty, therapy itself can help everyone. No matter where you are or how you feel, you can always benefit from seeing a therapist. I don't say this because I am a therapist. I say this in the most altruistic manner because everyone can gain something from getting another's perspective.

When seeing a therapist it's essential to know they don't have all the answers, and they aren't going to tell you what to do. Seeing a therapist is helpful because they can highlight some things we may have become so accustomed to that we don't even notice them anymore.

I will always remember the ah-ha! moment when I was seeing my therapist, Rebecca, in college. I had been dating this guy for a couple of years when our relationship suddenly shifted and began to feel more like a burden, and I couldn't figure out why. I didn't want to see him as often, and everything he asked of me seemed to take all the energy I had. I brought this issue to Rebecca, asking her what was wrong with me and what I could do to make it better. After explaining what had been going on in more detail, she merely repeated back to me what I had told her (to ensure she had heard me correctly, or so she said), and upon hearing my own words I suddenly saw the issue. Everything had to be done on his schedule, and I mean everything!

I was floored. I remember realizing that I was waiting hours after I became hungry to eat dinner because he would ask me to wait until he was done with work, sometimes until nine at night. I was also always the one to make the trek to his apartment; he would never come over to mine. Since these shifts didn't occur overnight, I didn't even know it was happening until it had been going on for over a year. Just having an outside voice shed light on the situation changed my life. It stopped me from continuing the relationship. It taught me that my time is valuable too, and that I have a right to an equal say in all my relationships.

It wasn't that Rebecca told me any of this directly, nor did she ever tell me to dump that loser and move on. All she did was reframe a situation I had been dealing with for over a year, and let me process through all that came up for me when she did. What I'm describing is what a therapist is supposed to do. Nothing more. A therapist shouldn't tell you what to do—that could cause you more guilt and shame. They should be unbiased and supportive as you come to the conclusions that are best for you at the time. This is all obviously said with the idea that the "therapists" I am referring to are good at their jobs and worthy of the opportunity to work with you.

How Much Help Do I Need?

Reaching out for help can sound nonspecific and unattainable, but after I explain what treatment options are out there, I hope you will know that you do have the ability to get the right amount of help when you need it most. Starting with seeing a therapist like myself. Traditionally, seeing a licensed therapist means you go to their office once or twice a week and talk about what is bothering you for fifty minutes at a time. This can be helpful if we are just not feeling like ourselves and need another, more useful perspective. This is the right level of care for you if the time in between sessions isn't so terrible that you can't manage. You should be able to get to therapy, try some of the tips your therapist offers, and moderately function in life. Again, we have to check in on how well we are doing with our daily to-dos and how we are feeling.

If you find yourself struggling to participate in therapy or do any of the tasks you are asked to try out of session, psychotropic medication (meaning medication for mental illnesses) can be another part of treatment. To find out which drug is right for you, you will need to make an appointment with a psychiatrist. They will ask you about your symptoms, how long the problem has been going on, and find what works best for you. Medication can take many weeks to show an effect, so do your best to be patient and give it the time to potentially work for you.

For many people, medication and therapy alone are not enough; there are more days than not when we just cannot do what we need to do each day. That is when we need to consider a higher level of care. What this means is that instead of only going to your therapy and doctor's appointments, then going home, you would spend most of your day in a treatment program.

Every treatment program is going to be different in how it structures each day, but overall there are group therapy sessions, you see your primary therapist one on one each week, and you also see a psychiatrist. It's a sort of one-stop shop where you receive all the treatment you need. Many programs have people come for just half of each weekday; others keep you for three full days a week; and some have you come all day each weekday. The highest levels of care (often called *inpatient*) have you stay at the facility full time. Yes, that means you sleep, eat, and receive all your treatment while living at the treatment home or hospital. Since I know making the decision to go into a hospital or inpatient facility can be incredibly scary for people, here is a story from a viewer who decided she needed that level of treatment, and why she felt that way.

> When I went into the hospital, I did so voluntarily. I knew I was heading downhill quickly. Over the years, I have learned what signs to look out for in myself, so that I can be proactive about getting help instead of waiting till it is too late. I was beginning to isolate myself from everyone around me, having obsessive thoughts of death (in general), and thoughts of wanting to hurt and/or kill myself. I couldn't concentrate at work or anywhere else for that matter. The people around me noticed that I wasn't quite myself, also. When that happens, it usually means I need to get some immediate and intensive help, or I will find myself in a bad situation.

I always advise people to consider how they are doing at each level, building up until they feel the support they are receiving meets all they need to fully function. The only reason we would need to jump right into a hospitalization would be that by the time we reached out for help, we already weren't functioning at all. This could mean we hadn't been eating, sleeping, or weren't even able to bathe ourselves. Many who have found themselves in this sort of a situation didn't know what to do about it; they've shared how they knew they didn't like how they felt but were afraid to tell anyone about it.

I hope that by talking about our mental health in a very open and nonjudgmental fashion we can shorten the time it takes people to speak up and get the help they need. No one deserves to feel ill for an extended period of time due to what they fear others will think of them. Together we will make sure everyone can get the help they need when they need it most.

How Do I Know If I Am Ready to Get Help?

I was just talking with my friend Nick about this question, because he has been in therapy off and on for many years and is pretty candid about his process. After discussing how important therapy has been and how he feels he should start getting back into it again, I asked him how he first knew he was ready for outside help. His answer wasn't simple. He had struggled with depression off and on, but after his first real therapist left him due to a career change, he decided he could do what he always did (not get out of bed and fixate on negative thoughts) or he could use the tools he had to help himself. He didn't like how he had been feeling and knew he needed to change if he ever wanted to get better. So he used the tools he had been taught while also searching for another therapist, and never looked back.

My process has been pretty similar, although my start in therapy was all thanks to my mom. When I was about twelve years old, she decided we all needed to get into family therapy. She felt there were issues we weren't talking about, and one of her friends had told her therapy could help. So we all went. My brother and dad immediately hated it, while I couldn't wait to go back. Shortly after that, my mom suggested I continue going on my own and since I had found it so beneficial, I did. Therapy has helped me recognize some of the unhealthy habits I engage in, while also challenging me to be more patient and communicative with those around me. It's a lot of really hard, soul-searching work, but I can without a doubt say it's due to therapy that I am where I am (as well as who I am) today.

I asked many of my friends, family members, and viewers to share their stories about the first time they reached out for help. It can be so scary, and we often put it off for years hoping we will magically start feeling better, but in the end, many find themselves at their first therapy appointment. So I asked them what pushed them to finally make that call and reach out. No matter how complicated the story or how long it took them to take the first step, they all got help for the same reason: they couldn't stand how they felt anymore.

> Growth is painful. Change is painful. But nothing is as
> painful as staying stuck somewhere you don't belong.
> —*Mandy Hale*

We have all been there, dreading each day, and feeling so uncomfortable in our own body and mind that we sometimes want to scream. We don't have to know where we want to be or how to get there; that's why we seek the help of a professional. While they can't tell us what to do, they can offer some structure and guidance so we can move toward a healthier and happier place. If you are wondering if you should see someone and get some help, chances are you should. Take that first step, and know that any investment in your own happiness will be worth it.

Why It's Important to Have Friends and Family

Socialization is where we get to try out the new tools we learn in therapy. That's why having a therapist as well as a support system is best. If we learn new ways to communicate in session but then never talk to anyone during the week, how will we know if the techniques are helpful? We won't. Having a one-sided relationship in therapy is supposed to help us see more clearly our own role in other relationships in our life, and help us work to improve them. If we don't have any social relationships, many of the goals in therapy will be focused on building our confidence to reach out and meet new people.

Another reason it's vitally important that we have relationships in our lives outside of our therapist or other professionals is that we as humans need love and connection. As children we are wired to connect, which is why our bodies are soothed by sucking, swallowing, and being held. All of these actions soothe our nervous system and pacify us. Sucking and swallowing are obviously calming because they help us bond with the person who feeds us. But more specifically, they reoptimize our heartbeats and breathing patterns, and regulate our digestive muscles, all of which help us feel more comfortable and soothed. Being held helps calm our amygdala (which prepares us for fight or flight) and is vital to our being kept safe from harm.[2]

I know a lot of this information may seem odd, but it's vital for us all to see why we need connection and how it can help

> The support of a mental health professional, as well as understanding from our friends and family, gives us the best situation for growth and healing.

us in our own healing process. In essence, connection is part of our development; it keeps us safe and helps us grow. Therefore, when we are struggling and don't feel like our true selves, having healthy relationships can help us move through it. The support of a mental health professional as well as understanding from our friends and family gives us the best situation for growth and healing.

What If I Don't Have Social Support?

Not all of us have loving and supportive families; many don't have a close friend with whom to share issues we may be having with our mental health. If we need more support, there are many other ways to get our needs met that don't include friends or family.

For starters, many schools have resources available to help out their students. All schools will offer some sort of counseling, but many offer group sessions. A private school I worked with employed two therapists to run an anxiety group each year, and I was able to refer a couple of my patients to it. There they were able to learn tools to better manage their anxiety symptoms, as well as connect with other classmates. This proved to be exponentially beneficial, since it was not just therapy but also a safe place to socially interact. Simply asking a teacher or school counselor for more information about their mental health services should give you an idea of what's available to you.

If your particular school doesn't offer things like that, many community centers do. One of my first internships was at a family community center where there were events, groups, and educational classes for anyone who needed them. Parents could come to get support, learn new skills, or just socialize with other people going through similar struggles. However, if your community seems to be lacking in extra services, there is always the online world. Between Facebook groups, meet-up sites, and the various peer support apps, there are many other ways to get social interaction when we need it.

I mention these other resources to let you know that wherever there's a need, we can find a way to meet it. I know looking for ways to help ourselves or those we love can sometimes be scary and even exhausting, but if we ask those around us, and do some simple online searching, we will find a way to get the connection we need.

Why Talking to Friends and Family Isn't Enough

Friends and family can be great. They can help us talk through issues at work and be there when we need to vent about our last relationship and why we think it went wrong. Having a support system is a great resource and something we should all have. I continually encourage my patients to make friends and reconnect with healthy family members to give them another outlet and support. The reason I believe friends and family are not enough to help us with our mental health is simple, really. Have you ever had that friend who likes to get in on the gossip, or egg you on when you are venting about a conflict? What about a friend who only talks about themselves and never asks you how you're doing? I am pretty sure you are nodding right now, because we all have those people in our lives, and although they can be great to talk to, they don't always know what to say or how to help.

While it's wonderful to have people who have known us for years, and we can vent about all that is going on, what they often do is agree, complain alongside us, and listen. They don't know how to softly guide us toward goals we have set or changes we want to make, nor is that what we should be asking of them. Sometimes all we want is for someone to nod along and complain with us, but that doesn't help us change or grow. That's why friends and family are great additions to seeing a mental health professional, but are not enough on their own.

Therapy helps move us along, challenges us when we need it most, and gives us a safe space to say things out loud. Yet on its own it's not enough either. In therapy the focus is all on you. There's no give and take; you don't have to ask your therapist how their week was. It's your time and yours only. In all honesty, that's what makes therapy so unique: it helps us finally focus only on ourselves without any distractions. That way we can hopefully begin to see ourselves more clearly and decide what we want and what we need to focus on.

I want you to know that you are not alone in your struggle. There are over forty million others in the United States alone who suffer from mental health issues,[3] and the more we talk about it, share our stories, and support one another, the better off we all will be. By having a better understanding of what symptoms and signs to look for in ourselves and in those we love, we can reach out and get help before it takes any more time from us.

Key Takeaways

- We don't have to fit the criteria for a mental illness to warrant getting help.

- Start tracking your mood and feelings each day so you can figure out what your norm is.

- Keep track (in any order) of three to five feelings you've had each day.

- Remember! Therapy can help anyone because it offers a new and unbiased perspective.

- If we get help and struggle a lot in between sessions, we may need further professional care.

- We are wired for connection and relationships. That's why a therapeutic relationship, as well as friends and family, will be a crucial part of our treatment and growth.

chapter 4

Mental Health Professionals Decoded

Who Does What?

It seems that every job comes with its own language and set of abbreviations or acronyms. It can be a shorthand way of mentioning a report that's due each week, or even an abbreviated term used to describe a job title. The mental health field is no different, and because there arc so many various professionals you can see when working on yourself, I am here to make sense of it all.

As someone in the mental health field, I feel that the number of job titles, differing degrees, and letters listed after a professional's name is dizzying. I often get asked what I do and when I give my full job title (I am a licensed marriage and family therapist), the response is usually "Oh, so you only see families and couples?" Since the answer to that is "No, I see all sorts of people and combinations of patients," there needs to be some clarification.

The degrees and licenses we acquire do begin to narrow down what we want to practice, and what our specialties are. However, our level of education doesn't necessarily define our careers or who we will treat in our office. It does, however, expand or limit who we can legally see, what we can say and do, and gives you an idea of who you should seek out for your specific issues.

Professionals are people too, who will have their own beliefs about treatment and what that should look like. Therefore, I merely describe the level of schooling they must go through, what they legally and ethically can and cannot do, and how their patients may perceive those differences. Think of this as your decoder for all those letters you see after someone's name. After reading through this chapter, you will be better able to create your treatment team, filled with professionals who can help you with whatever is upsetting you. I differentiate between the various clinicians in a general way, based on what you are most likely to encounter.

Psychiatrist

Let's start with the medical doctors. Psychiatrists are medical doctors who specialize in the treatment of mental illnesses. To become psychiatrists, they must complete a four-year undergraduate education as well as four years of medical school, after which they spend roughly four more years in residency (one of the final stages in graduate medical training). During residency they decide their specialty. This is where other medical doctors figure out that they want to work in pediatrics or be an ear, nose, and throat specialist. Psychiatrists decide they want to work in the mental health field, and they begin spending most of their time treating patients with mental illnesses. All of their medical training is why you will see the letters "MD" after their names. They are doctors who completed medical school and became licensed and possibly board certified.

The main difference between a psychiatrist and any other mental health professional is that psychiatrists can prescribe medication. Since they are medical doctors, they have the best understanding of medication, how it can affect our body, and what side effects we need to be aware of. That's why if you make an appointment to see a psychiatrist it could look something like this:

"Hello, Jane. Tell me what brought you in to see me today."
"Oh, I'm not really sure, but I have been feeling really down lately, and it seems to keep getting worse."
"Do you still find your usual hobbies enjoyable? Or have there been any changes in your appetite or sleep?"
"Yeah, I guess so. I haven't been eating very much, and I just don't want to write music right now. Also, I have been waking up really early and am unable to get back to sleep. What does all this mean?"
"To me, it sounds like depression. I am going to start you off on a low dose of an antidepressant, and I will check back in with you in a few weeks. It can take three to four weeks for you to feel the medication working, so be patient, but please let me know if you become suicidal or feel any other side effects. See you then."

That's usually it. An appointment with a psychiatrist is often fifteen to twenty minutes long, during which they focus on your symptoms and medication tolerance.

They used to see their patients for hour-long sessions and do therapy as well, but due to insurance pushback and cuts in reimbursement, psychiatrists mainly do what we now call *medication management.* It is because of this short, to the point, and dry interaction that most of my patients don't like them. It can feel cold, and as though they don't hear you. But they are a crucial part of mental health treatment. That's why I always ask my patients to write down all their symptoms and any questions or concerns they have. That way, even if the psychiatrist is speaking quickly and rushing through the appointment, they can still get what they need.

I know many of you have been reading this and thinking, "But, Kati, I see my general doctor for my antidepressant medication." While that may be true, I cannot stress enough how important it is that we see a medical doctor who studied psychotropic medication (that's what we call mental health medication), as well as all the signs and symptoms of mental illnesses. This ensures not only that we are correctly diagnosed, but also that we aren't put on medication that will make our symptoms worse.

A psychiatrist is the professional you see when you feel medication may be something you need. I always think of medicine as a safety raft in case we find ourselves drowning in symptoms. If we just don't have the energy or ability to attempt to use any of the tools or techniques our therapist offers us, then we are going to need something else to help get us well enough to give those new tools a try. Also, every psychiatrist is different; I know plenty who are warm and spend a lot of time with their patients.

Psychologist

Although a psychologist will call themselves a doctor as well, there's a significant distinction that needs to be made. A psychologist did not go to medical school and is not a medical doctor, and that's why they cannot prescribe medication for their patients. They have, however, completed their doctorate in psychology, which is why we call them doctors. Also, they did go through an exhaustive amount of schooling, completing their four years of undergraduate education, as well as an additional four years of graduate school. All eight years of their training were focused on psychology and treatment. After graduating, they then gather hours toward their licensing (it varies from state to state) and take the exam.

Psychologists either have a PhD (doctor of philosophy) or PsyD (doctor of psychology). And don't worry, most people are confused as to why there are two different degrees for the same thing, so let me explain. It wasn't until 1973 that PsyD programs were offered or recognized, but the reason for their development is very important.

Getting a PhD used to mean you focused on research and science as well as clinical application. Meaning that you not only learned about how to study people and their behaviors but also how to work with them to better their lives. As I am sure you can guess, that was just too much to cram into four years, and many felt that if the two were not separated, one area would always be neglected. So the two areas of study were split into separate education and licensing programs.

Therefore, a PsyD is the more clinical, in-office, working-with-patients program. Its focus is on therapy and spending time with patients, helping them work toward their goals. A PhD, on the other hand, is a more research, testing, and science-based program. However, because the PsyD has only existed since the early 1970s, and is not available in all graduate schools, many who have PhDs also do clinical work; there isn't any significant difference between the two. I am sure that will piss off some people, but as a patient of either of these types of professionals, you won't notice any difference in their ability to help you.

Another important distinction to make is that psychologists can offer testing and assessment, while many other mental health professionals cannot. This means that if you want to see if you have ADHD (attention deficit hyperactivity disorder), or just how severe your anxiety really is, a psychologist can administer the proper tests and interpret the results for you. Much of a psychologist's schooling focuses on testing and assessment, so they are the best option if you need any of those things done.

Psychiatric–Mental Health Advanced Practice Registered Nurse (PMH-APRN)

The most common way to encounter a psychiatric nurse is in a hospital. I used to work closely with PMH-APRNs during my time working at a local hospital's day treatment center. All nurses of any specialty have to begin their studies and licensure by becoming a registered nurse. There are various ways for someone to become a nurse:

- They can get an associate degree in nursing, which takes two years.

- They can get a diploma in nursing, which takes three years. These nurses usually work in a hospital setting; they can also get a bachelor's degree in nursing, which takes four years.

Graduates of these programs are eligible to take the registered nurse (RN) licensing exam and begin practicing as a nurse.[1]

Once they have completed their nursing degree, they must then earn either a master's or doctorate in psychiatric–mental health nursing.

What makes PMH-APRNs unique is that they not only have medical but also clinical knowledge. They are able to assess, diagnose, and in some states prescribe medication. What a PMH-APRN can do within their scope of practice really has to do with what advanced degrees they have completed. Many have private practices, while others work solely in the hospital setting. I found PMH-APRNs particularly helpful when they spoke to my patients about medication changes and what side effects they might feel, and made sure they were comfortable with their treatment.

Since there are so many variables when it comes to nursing, and because nurses can specialize in almost any treatment within the health field, it's important to ask them what training and schooling they have received. Whenever we are talking about specializations, I think it's vital that we ask any professional we see how they came to specialize in their field. In all honesty, you can even ask them to show you their résumé; that's entirely within your rights, and if you are concerned, just ask.

Licensed Marriage and Family Therapist (LMFT)

Yes, this is me. This is what I know most intimately. To become an LMFT one must first complete a four-year undergraduate program, usually majoring in psychology, but that's not a requirement. Then one must complete a two-year clinical psychology master's program. My program was called "Master's in Clinical Psychology with an Emphasis in Marriage and Family Therapy." All this really means is the program was geared toward clinical work with a focus on relationships. Much of my study was about therapy approaches and techniques, as well as how to verbalize what I was learning in session with a patient.

After graduating from the two-year master's program, LMFTs then have to accrue hours toward their licensing (just like psychologists). I am licensed in the state of California, which requires three thousand hours of clinical work. The state licensing board gives you six years after graduation to gather them, and it took me five; then I was eligible to take the two-part licensing exam. After passing both tests, we can technically call ourselves LMFTs and begin seeing patients on our own without supervision.

Like psychiatric nurses, LMFTs can specialize in various areas within the psychology field. When I first started looking for a job in my field, I was still in graduate school and needed something with supervision and pay. The only place that offered both was an eating disorder treatment center, and so I gratefully took the job. Due to that decision, I spent most of my training working with eating disorder patients; I learned all about the cause, treatment options, and recovery process of the disorder. That is why I can say with confidence that I specialize in the treatment of eating disorders; but I can't say as much for other therapists.

During my many years in practice, I have learned that therapists will say they specialize in various areas of psychology in which they have no formal training. You can find this out by browsing through your insurance company's list of covered therapists—therapists will list ten or more specialties, and I am here to tell you that you cannot trust a list like that. Not only is it not possible for a clinician to specialize in so many things at once, but I have found that many professionals will list every issue they have learned about so they can get as many new patients through the door as possible. Remember, being a therapist is a business too; that's why it's so important to ask questions and be informed. If it's specialized care we need, like addiction or eating disorder treatment, I would ask to see the therapist's résumé, or ask what training they have completed. I know this may sound harsh, but when we finally decide we are ready to see someone, we may have been suffering for years, and I just want to ensure you get the proper treatment when you need it.

LMFTs can treat many mental illnesses; they can diagnose and help you work toward your goals. And if properly trained, LMFTs can also offer some testing and assessment. Since our schooling is not primarily focused on that, we will need extra instruction and certifications. However, LMFTs cannot prescribe medication. Remember, only those who went to medical school (except for some RNs) can prescribe. It is a pet peeve of mine when therapists think it's appropriate to tell their patients what medication they should ask their doctor for. We did not go to medical school; we only have to take one class on medication, and we are not trained to offer that sort of advice. It's wholly and utterly wrong and is technically illegal, so make sure you get your medical advice from the right source.

As a final distinction, LMFTs are primarily trained to offer support and guidance in relationships. This could be the relationship you have with your spouse, friend, or even yourself. Our training is focused on helping you work better within all the groups you find yourself a part of, like work, family, and romantic relationships. We focus on how your emotional well-being affects those around you, and how we can help you feel more at ease within your environment. This will make more sense as we move on to the next type of mental health professional.

Licensed Clinical Social Worker (LCSW)

Social workers are much like LMFTs in that they finish four years of undergraduate education followed by two years of graduate school. They also tend to get their undergrad degree in psychology but then go on to a master's program for clinical social work. Upon graduation, they too gather hours toward licensure and must pass their exams in order to see patients without supervision.

The profession of social work has been around since the early 1900s and started as a way to aid those suffering from poverty, mental illness, disease, and much more.[2] I think it's important to know where social work started, because that has shaped how it's practiced today. Instead of focusing on how we are affected by those around us, or what our relationships are like, LCSWs' schooling emphasizes how to help you as an individual in your environment. That means that instead of concentrating on how you are doing in your relationships, they focus on getting you on the right track. They can assist you in preparing to get a job or help you overcome your test anxiety, as well as help you get the services you need to live.

Because of these things LCSWs tend to find work in government-run facilities, child protective services, or other agencies. They are the best at understanding how to help us function in our environment. We don't have to work through all those messy familial relationships from our past, but instead can focus on how we are doing and what tools we need to keep moving forward. In many ways, this approach can be very logistical and directive, but it can help those of us who may not have the ability to work through our past in order to grow and improve.

Here's the annoying part, though. I have many friends and colleagues who are LCSWs; we all finished graduate school, studied for our licensing exams, and began practicing around the same time. What I learned from that is that LMFTs and LCSWs can pretty much do the exact same thing. Even our exam prep courses were the same! I was shocked and also frustrated because it had taken me months to decide whether I wanted to become an LMFT or LCSW. Turns out, it doesn't really matter.

LCSWs can have their own private practice, and help you talk through your relationship issues; LMFTs can help you get the services you need to keep your mental and physical health at their best. When it comes to these two degrees and licensure, I honestly think it's more about the person you go to see. If you like them and they have the education and knowledge to help you with your issue, then I think you are in the right place.

Licensed Professional Clinical Counselor (LPCC)

LPCCs are the newest addition to the mental health profession. It may vary from state to state, but in California, where I practice, LPCCs were only added to the list of licensed clinicians in 2009 and no one was allowed to apply for a license until 2011.[3] A person calling themselves a "counselor" in the past could merely be someone who wanted to offer sound advice because they had been through it themselves, or because they felt they had some knowledge they wanted to share. Counseling wasn't regulated, and as a result people could reach out and not end up getting the care they really needed. So now it's monitored and governed by state licensing boards.

Just as you may have suspected, LPCCs have to complete pretty much the same requirements as LCSWs and LMFTs. No wonder everyone's so confused about what the various titles mean; licensing boards and educational systems do not clearly differentiate between many of the mental health professionals.

Nevertheless, LPCCs complete a four-year undergraduate program followed by a two-year graduate program. Then they too must acquire hours toward their license and pass their licensing exam.

LPCCs learn various therapeutic techniques and how to apply them, as well as how to accurately assess a patient. They can work with people who are adjusting to a disability, who want to focus on their personal growth, or who are managing a crisis. LPCCs cannot prescribe medication, but they can help you with any other emotional issue you may be struggling with.

Overall, LPCCs tend to take the broadest approach to helping their patients. They do not merely focus on relationships or ways to better navigate our environment, but instead look at our struggle more generally. They take in all the information we give them and work to help us in our personal growth and development using a variety of therapeutic techniques. As always, if you want them to help you with something specific and they say they specialize in that, feel free to ask them about their training and education to ensure they are the best fit.

Licensed Educational Psychologist (LEP)

You will only encounter an LEP if you are working in or with the educational system. Before someone can consider becoming an LEP they must have completed a four-year undergraduate degree, as well as a master's degree or higher. Then, after completing all their schooling and working in the educational system for at least three years, they must pass their licensing exam.

Once they pass their exam, the focus of their practice is all about education. LEPs can help assess and test for any mental health issue that may be affecting a person's ability to complete school work, and interpret the results of the tests so the person can better understand what the scores mean. They can also diagnose learning disabilities, and offer sessions with students and their parents in order to make sure all the student's needs are being met by the school.

I have worked with LEPs when fighting to get my patients individualized education programs (IEPs). They are the ones who make sure my patients' teachers know their individual needs, and they also ensure that their IEP is upheld. Usually, LEPs were school counselors before their licensure and went the extra mile in order to offer more assistance to their students. If the struggle you are facing has to do with schooling and getting more support during the educational process, LEPs can help you all along the way.

Why the Therapeutic Relationship Matters More Than Any Degree or Credentials

I know that I just spent a long time telling you about different degrees, levels of licensure, and specializations, but the truth is that none of that really matters if we don't connect with the person trying to help us. You could be seeing the best psychiatrist or psychologist in the world, but if you don't think they listen or care about you, then it's never going to work. Trust me. There have been enough studies about the importance of the therapeutic relationship that we could fill a whole house with it!

You could be seeing the best psychiatrist or psychologist in the world, but if you don't think they listen or care about you, then it's never going to work.

Therefore, know that once you feel that the professional you are seeing can legally and ethically meet your therapeutic needs, the only other thing that needs to be in place is that you like them and feel that they like you. Simple enough, right? Well, there's a lot more to it than that, but for the sake of this chapter, it's just important to know that you should like who you see. At least enough to feel that you can tell them things you don't regularly talk about, and that they hear you and want you to get better.

Would I Ever Need to See More Than One Mental Health Professional?

There are many reasons why someone would need to see more than one clinician. People often worry about what this might mean, or that they need to be even more "ill" in order to deserve well-rounded treatment. In my experience, about 75 percent of my patients are seeing me as well as another clinician, so know that you are not alone in needing to see more than one person.

The first and most common situation occurs when we need medication in addition to therapy. In that scenario, we would need to see a psychiatrist as well as utilize one of the many options for therapy (e.g., seeing an LPCC, psychologist, etc.). That way if we feel like we are drowning in symptoms, we can get help with medication as well as receive the tools and support we need through therapy.

Other than needing to see more than one professional due to medication management, the next most common scenario would be when we need a specialist for a particular situation. Many of my patients see me in order to learn tools and techniques to help them overcome their eating disorder, or even to help manage their anxiety level. However, if they have been through a trauma in their life, and no matter how much we talk about it in session it still doesn't get any better, I may refer them to a trauma specialist. I have only been trained on how talk therapy can help my patients process a trauma, so if they need a more intensive or different approach, they will need to see someone else.

When making a referral like that, it's important to discuss what this means. For example, why are we making the referral and why does my patient keep seeing both of us? First, the referral would be made because what my patient needs is beyond my scope of practice (meaning outside of my training and education). Second, they can keep seeing us both because the trauma specialist will solely work on the trauma, leaving the behavioral techniques and treatment goals to me. But if seeing two therapists seems like too much, and you would prefer to see only one, you can always visit only the specialist until you feel your work with them is done. Remember, your treatment is ultimately up to you, and you get to decide what you think is best. It's just good practice to talk about this with your therapist so you can hear their side as well.

There can be many reasons to see more than one mental health professional, including transitioning to a new clinician. This could be because they are moving their practice, or no longer seeing patients, or you don't feel it is a good fit. Whatever the reason, we find someone else and start seeing them so that we aren't without proper care. I find it's best if both professionals can be in contact with one another to share any relevant information as well as treatment goals; this way you don't spend a long time catching up the new clinician on your life and what you were already working on.

I know I say this a lot, but it's essential for you to hear that everyone's process is going to be different. I have patients who have five different health professionals they see as part of their treatment, while others only see me. What matters most is that you feel you are getting the necessary amount of support and guidance for where you are right now. If you are struggling to keep it together in between sessions, or maybe you feel that you are drowning in your symptoms—whatever the case—you can always ask for more help. That's why all these professionals went through all that schooling, hands-on training, and hour acquisition: they want to help those who are suffering and improve people's lives. So reach out, find what's best for you, and know that it can get better.

chapter 5

What Is Best for Me?

Finding the Right Kind of Therapy

Unfortunately, it's not just a therapist's schooling that can be confusing, but also the type of therapy they practice. Some say they are CBT based while others boast of being an EMDR therapist, and again we are lost in a sea of acronyms. Many professionals pick and choose from a variety of therapy techniques. However, it is essential to understand how those different treatments work and what problems they can help you with. This may come as a shock, but not all forms of therapy are the same, and many only work for those suffering from specific issues.

Over the years there have been hundreds of different types of psychotherapy, each professional finding some new way to help those struggling. In truth, it's not entirely about helping patients; mental health professionals have egos too, and it seems that everyone wants a treatment method named after them. Therefore,

> It's pivotal that we understand what valid options are available, and what works best in our specific case.

it's pivotal that we understand what valid options are available, and what works best in our specific case.

Some therapies focus on changing behavior, while others work on helping us heal from our past. The different names and descriptions of these options can be overwhelming, especially if you need help now and are trying to figure out who to see. So consider this your cheat sheet into the world of psychotherapy. I cover the most practiced and legitimate forms of treatment, talk a bit about how they came to be, and share the types of concerns they address best. In some cases, I walk you through how part of a session of a particular therapy could look and feel, so you can be prepared for your first appointment.

I focus on the therapies we see and hear about most. After reading through this chapter, you will be able to decipher the psychology mumbo-jumbo and feel able to make the right treatment choice.

Psychoanalysis

We might as well start at the beginning with the pioneer of psychotherapy, Sigmund Freud, who practiced at a time when the concepts of mental health and psychology were very new. Traditional psychoanalysis is based on the theory that all humans are driven by their instincts and biological drives; it focuses on looking into how our unconscious mind affects us each day. In Freud's time, much of what was used in a session was dream analysis as well as free association. (Free association consists of voicing thoughts without worry that they are coherent, logical, or appropriate.)

I start with psychoanalysis because it remains the foundation of the therapy we know today, and you will be able to see how other types of treatment are derived from portions of it. However, it is important to note that traditional psychoanalysis is not practiced much today, and for good reason. It can take years (and a ton of money) for you to complete it, which already limits who can benefit, not to mention that you don't look at the therapist while you talk. They are supposed to remain entirely detached from you and your process, to stave off transference. (Transference occurs when a patient transfers their feelings from a person or experience in the past onto their therapist.) Also, the focus on biological drives leaves out a lot of other reasons people act the way they do. Thus, this form of therapy isn't well supported and does not render favorable results.

As a way to make psychoanalysis more palatable and useful, many modern therapists have created briefer treatments and allow more interaction between patient and therapist. They have also turned their focus to the present issues at hand, rather than only working on childhood struggles. And instead of believing we are merely driven by biological needs, they recognize our ability to make rational choices. With all these changes in place, psychoanalysis can be beneficial to some. However, this is no longer a very common form of therapy.

Talk Therapy (Psychotherapy)

Even though Freud's theories didn't turn out to be entirely accurate, he did recognize that talking through issues with a professional was helpful. It's because of his work that we are able to benefit from modern talk therapy (a.k.a. psychotherapy). Many forms of mental health care fall under this umbrella term; however, since this is how most therapists market themselves, I want you to fully understand what it means. Talk therapy is pretty simple; its premise is that talking about the issues we are struggling with can help us feel better. It can allow us to clarify what we experienced, express what we think about it, and gain a new perspective.

Talk therapy is what I practice because it gives a therapist the ability to pick and choose different techniques from different treatments. It exists because every year there seems to be another type of therapy available that therapists would feel pressure to learn about, train for, and practice to the fullest extent. Instead of devoting our entire practice to a specific set of techniques, talk therapy allows us to learn about new forms of treatment and pick the tools and theories that best fit our patients and their needs.

Talk therapy starts with an intake appointment. You meet with the therapist, and while you try to decide if you like them, they will simultaneously try to get information about what's upsetting you. This is like an odd first date; your date doesn't tell you anything about themselves and instead asks you a lot about your life. I usually ask my patients simple things like "What brings you in today?" or "What's been going on that caused you to make this appointment?" That way you can tell me what's going on without my having to waste your time figuring it out. I also ask about any past treatments you've received, be it medication or other therapies, and how well you felt those worked for you.

After the intake appointment, the therapist will ask questions to ensure they understand the nature of your problem and how severe it is. Then you create a treatment plan together. A treatment plan is really just a guide to keep you on track. It can be a formal sheet you fill out together or merely notes on your goals, progress, and symptoms. Whatever it looks like, I firmly believe that all therapy should involve some form of treatment plan. This protects you as the patient, ensuring that you aren't wasting time and money. It's essential that we know what goals we are working toward, and that we periodically check in on how we are progressing. If your therapist doesn't talk about a treatment plan, they may prefer to keep it for their own reference, but know that you can ask them to share it with you.

The goal of talk therapy is to help you better manage the issue or disorder that brought you in. Then depending on the goals you have discussed with your therapist, you could also seek to resolve any past pain or work to find the underlying issue that caused it. That's what I love about talk therapy: you can work with your therapist in a variety of ways to make the treatment fit your specific needs. These next therapy styles are all methods a therapist may pick from to give you the best treatment they can.

Cognitive Behavioral Therapy (CBT)

I think it's safe to say that CBT is the most popular type of therapy out there today. CBT is a focused, short-term behavioral treatment that helps us see the link between our beliefs, thoughts, feelings, and actions. This means that how we act in certain situations is guided by our thoughts and not by what actually happened. Therefore, if we work to change our thoughts, we can change how we feel and act. The process of changing those thoughts is called cognitive restructuring, and the thoughts we want to restructure are those that are distorted and not based on facts.

When we feel depressed, we may think that nothing is ever going to go right and that we will always feel this way. That's why

CBT therapists believe that our distorted thoughts are like thick glasses we wear that prevent us from seeing the world in an objective and transparent way. CBT would be like going to an eye doctor and getting a proper prescription. You can finally see the world around you clearly.

CBT works by first having you notice which of your thoughts may be distorted. I use this technique—thought tracking—a lot with my patients. You keep track of your frequent automatic thoughts, write them down, and bring the list to your next appointment. The therapist then helps you recognize which ones are distorted or not, and teaches you how to argue back against the ones that are. This can help us stop black-and-white thinking as well as notice when we are turning a small issue into something much more substantial.

Since this type of therapy is short term and focuses on helping with a specific issue, it can be part of the treatment of many mental illnesses. The most common areas it works for are depression, anxiety disorders, insomnia, obsessive-compulsive disorder, eating disorders, and phobias. Done correctly, I believe CBT can help anyone, since we all have faulty thoughts and beliefs from time to time. Much of what your therapist will do with you in session is ask you questions to help get to the root of a falsely held belief about ourselves or situation.[1] Here's an example of what it could look like if you were worried about your upcoming presentation at work:

> "I just know that I am going to screw up my presentation at work. I am sure of it!"
> "If you screwed it up what would that mean?"
> "It would mean that I am terrible at my job."
> "If you are terrible at your job, what would that mean?"
> "That I am worthless and can't get anything right."

"What would it mean to be worthless?"

"It would mean that no one will ever love me, just like my
   mom always said."

That is obviously a shortened version of what could happen
in a session, but what CBT tries to do is get to the root of a distorted belief. In this case, it would be "No one will ever love me."
Once we have that information, we can help you see if you are
acting out of that belief, give you tools to notice when you are,
and help you do that less and less.

Dialectical Behavior Therapy (DBT)

DBT is a spin-off of CBT, and uses many of the same techniques
for fighting distorted thoughts and regulating our emotions. DBT
was created in the early 1990s as a way to help those who struggle with borderline personality disorder (BPD). Without having
to know precisely what BPD is, just understand that BPD causes
those who have it to feel everything in life very intensely, making
it tough to know how to manage or control the feelings that come
up when something upsetting happens. Therefore, the focus in
DBT is to offer tools to help us more quickly acknowledge our
emotions, where they are coming from, and know that we can
decide how to respond to them.

DBT is a very intensive treatment option, requiring patients
to have individual and group therapy sessions each week. They
must also complete homework assignments following each appointment. Having both forms of treatment in place is pivotal
to DBT working. DBT therapists believe that individual sessions
help keep suicidal thoughts and emotional issues out of the group;
a group is where you will learn all the tools unique to DBT, and

get a chance to practice them socially. DBT consists of four main modules: mindfulness, distress tolerance, emotion regulation, and interpersonal effectiveness.[2]

Over the years, DBT has been used to treat those with mood disorders (like depression or bipolar disorder) as well as those who are chronically suicidal. I use it in my practice to help those who struggle with eating disorders, substance abuse, and any self-injurious behavior. From inception, DBT was meant to validate and support patients who struggled to stay motivated in other forms of treatment, and thus the connection between therapist and patient is vital.

Sessions are filled with unconditional acceptance of a patient's feelings and experiences, while pointing out specific thoughts and behaviors that may be hindering their progress. When I practice this with my patients, much of our time together is spent managing any self-injurious actions, and any issues that may have come up in the group. I have my patients track their moods and unhealthy impulses, and we come up with healthier ways to cope with their waves of emotion.

I know the words "healthier ways to cope" can seem a bit vague, so here are a few examples. First, let's say that whenever we have a really stressful or bad day, we overeat. The urge to stop by our favorite fast-food restaurant pulls at us so intensely that it's the only thing we can think about until we finally give in. Afterward, we feel terrible about ourselves and think we have been very weak. In therapy we try to replace the unhealthy coping skill of overeating with other more healthy activities such as calling a friend to vent, putting all our stressful energy into a project we've been putting off, or even just creating a distraction from the stressful thoughts. Distraction techniques can be varied, from coloring or taking a bath to journaling or even going for a walk. We find that it takes about five healthy skills to replace the one unhealthy urge, so make sure you give at least five of them a try before you give in. Also, the longer we can put off unhealthy urges the more quickly they will go away. Here's an example from a viewer about her struggles with overspending.

I never thought my love for online shopping would be an issue, but when I lost my job it quickly became clear that I couldn't keep up with it anymore. I didn't have any credit left, and was barely making the minimum payments each month. I have never been so embarrassed in my entire life, and I was so depressed that my mom offered to pay for therapy if I would go. After fighting her on it for a while, I gave in, and it has been so helpful! Although it's really hard work, and I still overspend every so often, I now have a whole list of things I try to do before deciding to buy anything. Here are a few that have really helped.

1. Wait twenty-four hours. If I like something I have to wait to ensure that I really do love it and need it.

2. Journal about what's been going on that day or how I feel. I can also call a friend to vent if that's easier.

3. Distract myself from shopping by reading a good book or watching a good show on Netflix.

4. Get out of the house! I almost never spend money online when I am out with friends or even going for a walk.

5. Ask myself if I could pay cash for it. If the answer is no, then I can't afford it. I have to leave it in my cart.

I know I still have a long way to go, but I do feel like this list helps me not make such rash decisions only to regret them later. It has even helped me understand why I was spending so much in the first place, and now I know that I just need to talk about how I'm feeling instead.

In essence, we are trying to replace our urges to do harmful things with healthier behaviors. It takes practice and a lot of hard work, but with the right distraction techniques and tools you can find healthier ways to manage life's ups and downs.

Group Therapy

I want to briefly mention group therapy because it can be such a great addition to anyone's recovery process. Group therapy can be practiced in many various therapy styles, and for a wide variety of issues. I personally have run DBT groups, anxiety groups, and eating disorder recovery groups. It works so well because it not only allows us to learn from other people's experience but also continuously reminds us that we are not alone in our struggle. I also refer many of my patients to a group so they can practice using their new tools in a safe therapeutic setting.

Group therapy can be run by one or more therapists (depending on the size of the group), and usually follows a formula based on the issue at hand. Meaning that if we are working on our struggles with anxiety, the group leaders will use an anxiety workbook or particular style of therapy to guide them along week after week. There will be a method to each session, and homework assigned almost every week. Most groups also operate with a strict set of rules,[3] which usually include the following:

- *Confidentiality.* Anything said during group is entirely private.

- *Attendance.* By joining the group, you are committing to attend every meeting unless you have an emergency situation.

- *No cross talk.* If someone shares their story, you don't comment about it or state your opinion; you just listen and acknowledge their process.

- *Opt out.* No one is ever forced to answer a question or share something they don't want to share.

- *No violence, bullying, or intimidation within the group.*

- *No drugs or alcohol at group.* If inebriated, you are not welcome to participate.

- *No romantic relationships.* Starting or being in a relationship with someone in the group can create an uncomfortable environment; breaking up can make it hard for both members to continue, and since much is shared in the group, intimate issues might be brought up in group conversation.

- *Termination.* The group and therapist decide when and if someone should leave the group, or when the group ends. Keeping this all out in the open ensures that no one's feelings are hurt and that everyone is part of the process.

Group therapy works best as a supplement to individual therapy, unless you feel you are functioning well at the time and are merely looking for a way to get some support. Since you have to share time in a group and may have a week where you don't get to share, it can be hard if this is your only source of professional help. Therefore, when considering group therapy as an option, make sure you either have a personal therapist you see weekly, or you are only looking into a group format as a way to connect with others going through a similar issue.

Family Therapy

Family therapy was a necessary addition to the therapy world since merely working on ourselves doesn't seem to fix how we interact with those we live with. I think we all can agree that much of what we struggle with now can be traced back to something that happened earlier in our life, or a pattern of being in our family. That could be the reason we are always the one who keeps the peace, or maybe we are the one who expresses anger for everyone else in the family. Whatever it is, by participating in family therapy we can see the part we play in the system and how we can make it more harmonious.

Just like group therapy, family therapy can be practiced using various therapy techniques, and each person is given their own time to talk. It should also be a supplement to individual treatment where needed. The difference between group therapy and family therapy is that family therapy's focus is on how the family unit functions together. The idea of the family acting like a system, all parts working together to make it functional or dysfunctional, is called the family systems theory. What this means is that we each play a role in our family, and all players work together to keep the family afloat. This can be good or bad, but the overall goal of family therapy is to recognize our own role, whether or not it's helpful and healthy for the system, and change our behavior as needed.

I like to think of families as participating in a dance. When there's disharmony, it means that our dance is hurting one if not all members of the family; maybe we're stepping on toes and bumping into each other. This usually presents itself via the scapegoat: one member of the family who bears the symptoms of all the others. This could be a child struggling in school so badly that they fail out, or a parent cheating on their spouse. Even though many people see these as individual problems, a family therapist would work to figure out what is happening in the system to support such harmful behavior. Once they are able discover each person's role in the unhealthy behavior, they begin to challenge each member to act differently, and report back as to whether or not the new behavior changed their dance.

As a result, family therapy can be beneficial for many issues, as it helps build up and support the whole system. It is considered the second most effective form of treatment after CBT, and is most helpful to families with alcohol dependence, bipolar disorder, eating disorder, and schizophrenia.[4] I believe these are the mental illnesses it works best with because each of these issues requires the entire family's support to recover fully.

Exposure Therapy

The name of this therapy seems to send people running the other way. It sounds like you are going to be forced to face your fear whether you like it or not, but trust me, that's not the case. The truth about exposure therapy is that it's the best treatment for any phobia or worry, it's short term, and you rarely need to come back. In essence, it's your best option for finally kicking that fear of flying, spiders, or whatever.

When we fear something, it's natural for us to avoid it. However, if the thing we worry about keeps popping up and we continue to fight to keep away from it, then our phobia only gets worse. Facing the things we fear actually makes them go away (as counterintuitive as that sounds), and that's why exposure therapy works so well.

The first task when starting this type of therapy is to find some relaxation techniques that work for you. These could be things like breathing techniques, meditation, coloring, you name it. Just make sure they're useful, and can calm you down as you work toward facing your fear. Second, you will create a hierarchy of your anxiety as it relates to the phobia. Meaning that zero would be you at your most relaxed, and at ten you would be completely overwhelmed and shut down. This will give you and your therapist an idea of where to start in your treatment.

In the session, you will begin by visualizing yourself doing something related to the scary thing, and then working to calm yourself down. Once you feel calm, you slowly move back into the frightening situation. We do this over and over as a way to build up our ability to calm ourselves down. The goal is to do or face the thing we were most fearful of. What ends up happening is we learn that what was once so scary isn't really that scary after all.

Exposure therapy can be paced in many different ways, depending on what you and your therapist decide. Some people prefer the gradient way like I described above, while others want to jump right into it. As always, trusting your therapist and feeling safe in the office with them is an essential component to making treatment a successful experience for you.

Since exposure therapy was created to help people confront and overcome their fears, it has been scientifically proven to help those suffering from panic disorder, generalized anxiety disorder, post-traumatic stress disorder, phobias, social anxiety, and obsessive-compulsive disorder.[5]

Eye Movement Desensitization and Reprocessing (EMDR)

EMDR is a very nontraditional form of therapy that utilizes eye movements as a way to help us process through past trauma. Whether or not this is a viable form of treatment is still up for debate, but over twenty thousand mental health professionals have been trained in it, and it is currently supported by the American Psychiatric Association, the Department of Veterans Affairs, and the Department of Defense, as well as other organizations around the world.[6]

Why EMDR works continues to be researched, but it is believed that rapid eye movements help our brain process through an experience it may not have been able to deal with at the time the event occurred. During sleep we have periods of REM (rapid eye movement); it is believed that during this time our brain processes through all we've done during the day. Thus, if we instigate more rapid eye movement time into our day, we are giving our brain more opportunities to work through events. But that's just a hypothesis thus far; there is still more research to be done.

EMDR was created as a way for people to process through traumatic or distressing events. Therefore, it's suitable for those with post-traumatic stress disorder, or anyone who has sustained an overwhelming or painful life experience. Just like group therapy and family therapy, EMDR is also a supplement to individual treatment, since it's short term and trauma focused.

To initiate the eye movements, EMDR clinicians may instruct you to do different things. They may have you follow their finger or a light from left to right, tap you on your left and right sides, have you hold buzzers in your hands, or have you listen to beeping in your ears. The movements need to be from left to right for it to be considered EMDR, and most importantly, for it to be effective.

Once you have settled into your session, your therapist will start the eye movements, ensure you feel safe, and ask you to describe the distressing event. If you begin to feel overwhelmed, they will guide you out of the situation and into one that is more positive, to keep you present and not retraumatize you. This back and forth will continue as you get the chance to process through the painful memory, always ending the session on a positive recollection.

I have referred many patients for EMDR treatment, and they have had positive results. The first time I referred someone, it was because we had talked and talked about the abuse my patient sustained growing up, but she wasn't getting any better. No matter what I did, or how much homework she completed, the past abuse continued to affect her on a daily basis. We were both working very hard without any positive outcome. As a therapist, it is ethically required of me to look to outside resources for help when what I am able to do doesn't seem to be enough.

After a few months of EMDR, my patient was finally free of her past. She was able to talk through the traumatic events without having a panic attack or a flashback, and was eventually able to move on. Obviously, everyone is different, and there is still much to learn about EMDR, but if you find yourself stuck, it's nice to know this option is available.

Art and Music Therapy

It will probably upset some people that I put these two types of therapy together, but the goal of this chapter isn't to stroke egos but to help you understand the different therapy types. Art and music are both ways we communicate. Take a look at a work by your favorite artist, read the short description they gave for the piece, and you will feel what they were going through when it was created. The same goes with music; the lyrics, pacing, and even the instruments used can express so much emotion. Many people are better able to communicate how they feel using the mediums of music or art, and that is why both types of therapy exist today.[7]

We may often feel stuck in therapy, trying to find words to adequately describe what's going on inside us. It can be frustrating, and in some cases even cause us to quit, believing therapy just isn't going to work. Art and music therapy help give us another way to express ourselves so we don't feel alone or stuck. People often reference these two types of treatment when talking about children, but there is no age limit when it comes to either of these modalities. We can all benefit from having a healthy outlet for our emotions, not just children.[8]

Using art or music to express our struggles can be helpful in and out of therapy, but for someone to use either medium to aid in your recovery, they need to have gone through specific training and be duly certified. Just like I mentioned earlier, it's entirely acceptable to ask a therapist what training they have, and whether they are accredited. It is your time, money, and mental health, after all.

Since these forms of treatment can be so soothing and expressive, they are known to help those suffering from the following:

- Depression

- Anxiety

- Post-traumatic stress disorder (PTSD)

- Substance dependency

- Attention deficit hyperactivity disorder (ADHD)

- Dementia

Art and music therapy can be practiced in group or individual settings, and while you do have complete freedom of expression, the therapist will instruct and guide you to ensure that what you are working on is focused and therapeutic. Usually, a subject, experience, or issue will be the focus of the session (or sessions), and you will be asked to think of that while creating music or art. One of the main limitations of art and music therapy is that neither will work if we are not entirely invested and take the treatment seriously. There is no need to be an artist or musician to benefit; all that's needed is an open mind.

Doing What Feels Right

I left out many therapies because they are either redundant or not widely practiced. If you still find it hard to fully understand the different therapy styles, just remember that it's more about feeling comfortable with your therapist, trusting that they are there to help you, and wanting to get better. Also, if you have questions, you can ask your therapist. I promise you it is completely fine to ask them what it means when they say they use multiple therapies, or whether or not they are trained to treat your eating disorder. You are trusting them with your mental health; the least they can do is let you know whether they are qualified or not. You wouldn't go in for heart surgery without knowing that your doctor was in fact a cardiac surgeon, so why take a risk when it comes to your overall mental health?

chapter 6

Preparing for Your First Appointment

What to Expect and Questions to Ask

Now that we have figured out what type of mental health professional would be best, and what kind of therapy we need, the next step is making our first appointment. Doing anything for the first time can be scary because there are so many unknowns. Will I like them? What kinds of questions will they ask? What if I suddenly don't have anything to say? After all the years I have been a practicing therapist, and in my own therapy, I can honestly tell you that there is nothing to fear. Yes, it can be hard to say some things out loud for the first time, and if you're like me, you cry every session, but there's no reason to be scared. A therapist is there to hear you, put together some goals, and help you work toward them. Everything else is just logistics. Don't worry, I will walk you through those as well.

Setting up an appointment usually means you have to leave your prospective therapist a voicemail. Sure, some therapists have an assistant or an office manager, but most don't. Preparing for this call can relieve a lot of stress and anxiety, and ensure that you do in fact leave a message and set up the appointment you are needing. You don't have to tell them your whole life story or give a detailed description of all your symptoms, but you will need to let them know a few specific things.

First, let them know your full name and age. I know this sounds a bit obvious and silly, but you would be surprised how many people call me without telling me either of those things. Age is important because some therapists only see specific age groups in their practice; for example, I only see adult patients. Second, briefly tell them what's going on and how long you've been dealing with it. I always tell my viewers to stick with their symptoms, not the story. Here is an example of what that could look like.

> Hey, Kati, this is Sally, and I am a thirty-eight-year-old
> female looking to see someone about what I assume is
> anxiety. For the past few months I have been feeling my
> heart race, and I struggle to catch my breath sometimes.
> It is at its worst when I am at work or out with friends.
> I saw my doctor last week about it, and he recommended
> I see a therapist.

Telling them what's bothering you and how it feels can help the therapist decide if they are suited to treat you. Also, depending on how long it's been going on, they can begin to assess the proper level of treatment needed. During your fifty-minute session, you will have time to tell them all the details surrounding it, so the voicemail should be succinct.

Next, we have to talk about money so you are prepared and able to afford treatment. Do you have insurance? Do you want to use it? Does the therapist take that insurance plan? This is also a great time to ask them what they charge, and if they work on a sliding scale. (*Sliding scale* is a term we use to describe paying less than the full fee. It's an amount negotiated between patient and therapist.) I know that many of us can get squeamish at the mention of money, especially if we need to talk about it and possibly negotiate, but it's best to know the cost up front. That way we don't end a session and then find out it cost $300! Also, it can be easier to discuss this over voicemail or the phone versus in person, so doing it first thing is best.

Last, give them some days and times that could work for an appointment and the best way to contact you. If you are giving them a phone number that isn't solely yours (like a house or work line), I would also tell them whether or not it's okay to leave a message. That's it! I know this can sound and feel like a lot, so I have put together another example that is a continuation of the previous one. Feel free to copy both of these entirely if needed; they're here to help.

I have Blue Shield insurance, and while I would love to utilize those benefits, if you're not in network, I am happy to pay out of pocket depending on your fee. Please let me know what your hourly rate is. Thanks! I have Tuesday and Thursday afternoons and evenings free for sessions. Please call me back at this number, 555-7230, and feel free to leave a message. Thank you so much!

What Does an Actual Therapy Appointment
Look Like?

First therapy appointments are sort of like one-sided dates. Some simple paperwork is left in the waiting room for you that asks fundamental questions about you, the issue that brought you in, and whether or not you have been in therapy before. Once that's filled out, you let the therapist know you are there, usually by pressing a button (a light then coming on in our office is one way that lets us know you are there and ready for your appointment). Then the odd date begins. The therapist will go through the paperwork with you, asking questions where clarification is needed, and try to get a better idea of who you are and how they can help. I know these are broad statements, but each therapist is going to be different. Just as we discussed in the previous chapter, some will focus on your relationships, others on your ability to function in your environment. To give you some insight into what a first appointment looks like with me, here is an example:

Me: "Thank you so much for coming in and filling out that paperwork. I would like to go through it with you now if that's okay."

Patient: "Sure."

Me: "Great. It looks like you want some help with feelings of loneliness and possible depression. Does that sound about right?"

Patient: "Yes. I have been crying a lot for what seems like no reason, and recently even getting to work on time just seems impossible. I want to get this under control before I lose my job or get in trouble at work."

Me: "I completely understand, and we will work to get you feeling better as quickly as possible. You also wrote down that you have been in therapy before. Can you tell me a little bit about that, like what caused you to reach out then, and why you decided to stop going?"

Patient: "Yes, I have been in therapy before, but it was about eight years ago. My mom thought I should go when I was transitioning from college to work, and I was feeling down then as well. It was helpful at first, but I just never really clicked with them. So I thought I would try someone new this time."

Me: "I understand. I am glad you got support when you needed it, but you're right, you want to feel the click and like seeing them. That's honestly what makes therapy work."

That dialogue gives you an idea of how a first therapy appointment sounds and what types of questions you can expect. Overall, here is the best thing we can do in that first session: be honest. I always tell my audience and patients that a therapist can't help you if they don't know what's going on. By giving us as much information as you feel comfortable with, you allow us to use the best skills and tools to help you. Without it, we could be giving you tools that aren't helpful, and even thinking you are doing better than you are.

If you are nervous that you may clam up and not be able to tell them anything, it can help to practice what you want to say ahead of time. I know that talking to yourself sounds crazy, but saying things out loud for the first time can be scary, so doing it alone first can take the edge off and help you feel comfortable with it. Also, I recommend writing down the essential things and bringing the list with you to your session. What I mean by the "essential things" are your symptoms, biggest struggle, and what you want to get out of therapy. With those three things, any therapist should be able to get an idea of whether or not they are your best option and begin to put together a treatment plan.

What Should I Expect to Get Through in That First Appointment?

It's also important to know that first appointments can go by very quickly. It can feel like you barely got to tell the therapist anything, and your time is up. If that's the case, make sure you keep bringing in your list and practicing what you want to say beforehand, until you feel you have said what needs to be said. The amount of information you will be able to share with them depends on how quickly you can talk about it. I have what has been called "diarrhea of the mouth" because I cannot get it all out fast enough. I may ramble for forty minutes straight until my therapist stops me and inserts some helpful tools and tips. Other people struggle to share anything, so know that it's okay to go at the pace that feels comfortable for you. This is your therapy and your process, and it needs to be done at your speed.

Many of my patients have asked me why it's only a fifty-minute hour. Some are even upset that they pay me "by the hour" yet they don't get the final ten minutes. The reason therapy runs in fifty-minute increments is logistical. There are things we need to do in between seeing patients, and if our schedule is fully booked, there needs to be time to squeeze in those to-dos.

Therapy isn't like an oil change or haircut; it doesn't end promptly, and therefore that extra ten minutes allows us a few minutes to wrap up our conversation, get payment, take any notes we need to about the session, and possibly go to the bathroom if we need to. There is a lot that goes on in between sessions, and I am sure I'm not the only therapist who may also try to squeeze in a snack too. In all truth, ten minutes isn't enough, and that is why therapists often run behind schedule. So don't think it has anything to do with you, or that the therapist isn't going to give you your full time; we may just be trying to scribble the last of our notes from our previous session, or finish that granola bar we brought from home.

Why You Need to See Someone More Than Once

I know that by the time we pick someone to see, make the appointment, and get up the courage to go, it can be utterly disheartening if we don't enjoy meeting them. There can be a lot of pressure on first appointments, and as I said earlier, the sessions fly by. Therefore, it's important to see a therapist a few times before deciding whether or not they are the right fit.

The first session will be filled with questions about you and your past, as well as what's going on in your life now. Since that's a lot of information to cram into fifty minutes, it often continues into the next few sessions. Just like meeting a new friend or going on a first date, it can take us a bit of time to decide whether we like them and want to keep seeing them. Therapists are people too, and they can have hard days or be distracted, but that doesn't mean we should immediately shelve the idea of working with them. The process of deciding whether or not someone is a good fit can take some time, and be hard to conceptualize, so here's an example from one of my viewers:

> The first several sessions were extremely hard, and I
> left feeling overwhelmed. I associated the way that I felt
> after a session with her, and that kept me from being
> sure whether it was a good fit or not. Even though I

liked her, thought she was very nice, and felt I could talk to her about most things, I still wasn't entirely sure that I wanted to continue with our sessions. After a few months, I ultimately decided that therapy was helping me even though it was hard work. I am so glad that I pushed through the rough beginnings those first few months because it gave me time to really get to know my therapist and feel that she gets me.

You can see that in this case, it took the patient a few months to decide she wanted to keep seeing her therapist, so know that everyone's process is going to be different. Like I said before, we just need to make sure we like them so far, like talking to them, and feel they are on our side fighting with us.

In my experience, it's been pretty easy to find someone I like. Not because I immediately loved and knew I wanted to keep seeing each therapist I went to see, but because throughout the years I have gotten pretty good at reading people. I can usually tell if someone is authentic or bullshitting me and whether our personalities are going to meld well together. Taking those things into consideration, and treating my potential therapist as if they want to be my friend, have really helped me find a good fit. If you don't feel you can do that quickly, here are some things to consider after or during your first appointment:

1. Do you feel comfortable talking with them? Even though what you are talking about can be difficult and unnerving, do you still feel you can push through?

2. Do you like the way their office feels? This may seem like a small thing but can really make a difference when it comes to opening up and getting the most out of your sessions.

3. Do you look forward to going to therapy? I know that it's backbreaking work, and sometimes we may not want to do it, but overall it's important that we don't mind going. Even if it's only so we can finally talk to someone about everything that's been going on.

Hopefully, those three tips will help you feel better able to find the right therapist. I know it can be scary, but it's important to trust your gut when finding someone to work with. Whether or not we want to admit it, we know when we do and do not like someone. Put those feelings to good use, and you will end up with a great therapist who can help guide you toward your goals.

Boundaries and Ethics in Therapy

Entire books are written on this topic alone. But for the sake of time and not boring you to death, I will just let you know how boundaries and ethics apply to you in therapy. First, it's important to understand that a therapist cannot be reachable at all times. That may sound obvious, but some people seem to think we are on call 24/7 like medical doctors, and we are not. If you have an emergency you do need to contact us, but it may take us several hours to get back to you. That's why most mental health professionals will have you go to a hospital or call 911 if you are in danger.

We shouldn't know too much about our therapist's personal life. Knowing too much about them can change the way we see them in therapy, and what we may feel comfortable telling them.

Other than emergency situations, contact in between sessions should be minimal. This is because the entire goal of therapy is to get you feeling good and making healthy choices on your own. Although different mental illnesses and therapeutic specialties will require differing amounts of time for treatment, overall the goal is that you won't need treatment anymore. Also, maintaining a boundary of contact in between therapy sessions ensures you perceive your therapist as a professional rather than just a friend. That may sound harsh, but remember earlier when I talked about how different a friendship and a therapeutic relationship are? It's for those reasons that we need to see our therapist as a professional specialist and guide.

We shouldn't know too much about our therapist's personal life. Knowing too much about them can change the way we see them in therapy, and what we may feel comfortable telling them. For example, if we know our therapist goes to a specific church, and we don't believe in the same things, it could make talking about our beliefs hard or uncomfortable. It could cause us to discontinue our treatment with them even if we felt things were going well. We want to keep therapy about you, and not about your therapist or what they choose to do outside the office.

As therapists we are taught to be as unbiased as possible in our practice. Meaning that we need to keep any judgment or beliefs outside so we can listen to our patients and help them in the best way for them and their life. This could be concerning religious beliefs, political beliefs, or even lifestyle choices. It's not a therapist's job to tell you what is wrong or right for you. They can only highlight any concerns they have, listen to your thoughts and beliefs about them, and help you work toward your goals.

Since we are paying a therapist to sit with us, listen, and help guide us toward our goals, we also need to hold them accountable, making sure they keep regular appointments with us, hear us when we talk, and remember what goals we are working toward. All of this may sound very obvious, but you would be surprised how many of my viewers have reported unethical practices. Here's one:

> My wife and I were seeing a therapist that not only
> forgot details, he forgot my wife's NAME . . . over and over
> and over through several sessions he would call her
> the wrong name, and not always the same wrong name.
> We gave him the benefit of the doubt for too long. Right
> before we dropped him, I lost my cool with him and
> raised my voice: "You've got a legal pad in your lap . . .
> *write it down!*"

It's completely acceptable to expect your therapist to remember your name. They should also be awake during your appointments, follow along as you talk, and ask clarifying or guiding questions throughout. I know much of that goes without saying, but since I regularly hear horror stories like the one above, I want to make sure everyone knows what's okay and not okay.

Just as in every job out there, some people are good at what they do and others are not; mental health professionals are no different. We are human, and can have off days or times when we aren't feeling well. But overall we should be present with you, offering tools and techniques where needed, and simply doing our job.

How to Know You Are Seeing a Bad Therapist

Over the years I have realized just how mysterious the practice of therapy is. Many people will work with what I deem a "bad therapist" for years, and not know why they don't see any improvement. Others reach out to me to see if what their therapist is doing is normal or something they should be concerned about. Not talking about therapy or what we can expect, and how to know when it's right or wrong, is unacceptable. When we finally reach out for help, we need to know how to gauge whether that support is ethical and working for us. That's why I want to share with you some red flags that could indicate you are seeing a lousy therapist.

First, they don't remember anything you tell them. Just like the viewer's story I shared, many bad therapists will not even remember the names of their patients or influential people in their lives. This is entirely offensive and doesn't help build trust in the therapeutic process. At first you may have to repeat the names of your friends or family members as your therapist gets to know you, but after the first few reminders, they should remember. I know this may be considered old school, but I still handwrite all my notes. This allows me to jot things down during sessions, like names, ages, and how you are related to certain people. Most clinicians type everything out, but it's not too much to ask that they take some small handwritten notes during session so they remember essential details. If they don't, and they can't recall specifics, they don't deserve your time or money.

Second, they talk about themselves the entire time. You would be surprised how many therapists do this! They will take up your time in therapy to share how they struggled with that same issue, or how they used to have a friend just like you, etc. My mother was trying to find a new therapist, and after four or five sessions she asked me if it was normal for a therapist to share their own story. I was appalled! While a therapist may offer a small story about themselves to help you know they understand and can empathize with your situation, any more than that isn't ethical.

Remember, therapy is your time. This is the one relationship that is supposed to be all about you, your concerns, issues, and how to make you feel better.

Third, they downplay your issues or traumatic events in your life. You should never feel that you have to prove anything to your therapist; they are supposed to be on your side. I know many mental illnesses can cause us to worry that we aren't "sick enough" for help, but once we have support, the person we see should validate how we feel and work with rather than against us.

I recently taught a continuing education class to other therapists about self-injury. While preparing my presentation I realized that much of what a therapist does is listen, so why not look to my audience and see what they would like their therapist to know about their struggles with self-injury. I received hundreds of responses, but this one stood out:

> Don't downplay the level a person chooses to self-harm
> (e.g., scratching is just as damaging in a sense as cutting
> or burning, etc.). "Oh, was it just scratching you did?"
>
> The power of the word stays with a patient more than
> any advice you may give.

This statement can apply to a lot of different issues, whether it be your feelings of depression or even the state of your marriage. Never let a therapist act as if your problems don't warrant help. That's a sign that they are terrible at their jobs; they shouldn't be taking on new patients if they don't want to help them.

Fourth, a therapist should not be accessible to you at all times. What I mean by that is they shouldn't allow you to text or email them anytime you want to, except for an emergency. Like I mentioned before, this is important so that our relationship with our therapist is healthy and we are given a chance to try things out on our own. If we feel we can always count on our therapist to get right back to us when we're having a hard time, we won't be able to figure out how to function when they aren't there. No one but ourselves can be there around the clock to ensure we make healthy decisions; relying on someone implicitly for our recovery is not the goal of therapy.

Fifth, there is no end of therapy in sight. I know there are many ways to practice therapy, but regardless of the style, they should all work toward an end. You should have goals that you talk about and write down; you can even create smaller goals that lead you in the direction you're heading. If you find that your time in therapy is spent catching up and chatting like old friends, it is no longer working. A good therapist will let you know when your work together is finished, and talk about it with you. You should jointly decide to stop meeting weekly or biweekly and see how it goes, knowing you can always return to therapy when you need to. When treatment turns into a lighthearted chat without any focus or benefit, it's not therapy anymore.

The sixth sign is that your therapist tells you what to do. I know you may think I am lying to you, but it's not a therapist's job to make choices for you. We could each have a different way of dealing with a situation, and that doesn't make one choice right and another wrong. Every decision you make together in therapy should be based on how you feel, and what you believe to be right, and keep in mind your goals. Sure, a therapist can guide you toward things they may think will help you or heal a relationship, but in the end you get to decide. A therapist who pushes you to do things the way they say isn't a therapist; they are a bully and completely unprofessional.

The seventh red flag is that you never feel like a priority. We all know that our therapists see other patients and have their own life, but we shouldn't feel they don't care about us or our progress. This can happen when sessions are continually canceled or rescheduled, making it hard to know when we will see them next. Although people can get sick or have family emergencies, it's vital that we know we can count on our therapy time. Even if it's not the same day and time each week, we need to know we will get in to see them with some regularity.

The eighth and final red flag is not being given much if any feedback in session. If we are doing our best to share what we are feeling and what we have been through, our therapist needs to actively listen to us. They should nod, ask questions where needed, and guide us to see connections we may have missed. If your therapist is sitting there writing on their legal pad, or typing on their computer and not giving you any indication that they are listening, they probably aren't, and that's not okay.

I know that focusing on all the ways a therapist can be terrible at their job doesn't instill trust or excitement about the process, but it's imperative that we know what to look out for. This way we can ensure that when we do get in to see someone, we are aware that they are doing their job and we are getting the right help.

Ways to Know You Are Seeing a Good Therapist

In the same way we need to know what makes a therapist bad, we also need to talk about the traits or signs that we have in fact found a good one. Since there is so much confusion around therapy and what we can expect when we finally go, I get questions about all sorts of techniques therapists use. I will try to include as many signs as I can, and even give some examples of how it may look or feel in session because if you don't know this already, I really want you to look into therapy. I think it can help anyone feel better, and as a mental health professional, I really want people to feel good.

First, it's vital that you feel your therapist is on your side, wanting you to do well, and that you can trust them. This may go without saying, but it can be hard to open up at first, and feeling that they care and want to see you do well can make all the difference. It also helps build a healthy therapeutic relationship, which is pivotal to your being able to work with them. This first sign can be expressed through their getting excited when you meet a goal or overcome an obstacle. It could also be shown through supportive words when you're coming up to a stressful time, or reminding you that you are working on this together. You may even feel this yourself in your increased ability to open up and feel safe with them. My patients will often report this after the fact, sharing that they haven't told anyone that story before, or that they liked how I responded to them sharing something so private.

Second, they clearly communicate to you about the therapy process and what they are focusing on. There shouldn't be any air of mystery when it comes to therapy; everything should be discussed and decided upon together. This is important not only for the entire treatment process; communication is such an issue for many of us that being able to practice clear communication in the therapy setting is paramount to our feeling better overall.

Clear communication would mean that if you were to text or email your therapist about something that wasn't an emergency, they would bring it up in session so you understood why they didn't respond. They would also speak clearly with you about your treatment plan, goals, and what you were working on together. Being able to have an open conversation in therapy is important because it gives us a chance to let our therapist know what we want, how we feel, and if we agree with their treatment choices. Without this positive trait, therapy can be a waste of our time and even possibly cause us to believe that not talking about difficult issues is normal, which it is not.

Third, they challenge you. They don't push you past the limit of what's okay and safe, but they do challenge you to try something new, or move past some discomfort. Therapy is tough work and is entirely worth it, but it's not easy to work on ourselves. That's why seeking out treatment to make some personal changes is best. In the same way that you would get a trainer if you had a fitness goal, you can get a therapist to help you with your psychological goals. We need that trainer (or therapist) to encourage us, while also pushing us to do a bit more than we would on our own. If your therapist lets you off the hook quickly and doesn't challenge you to try again or tell them a little bit more, they aren't acting like a therapist.

I do want to add that a therapist shouldn't push you to a breaking point, like a panic attack or into a flashback. That's why I put this positive trait after the first two. They need to know what you can tolerate, challenge you when needed, but also be aware of your limits. You should feel comfortable letting them know when you have reached your max; that way you can learn together and work harder only when it's safe for you.

The fourth way to know that you are seeing a good therapist is that they help you better express yourself and your symptoms. Having the right words to express what we may be going through can be freeing and validating. This is my favorite thing to work on with patients, and I assume it's because it allows me to be a detective trying to find the right words to help them feel more understood; it's like solving an emotional puzzle. You will most likely hear your therapist say things like "Are you saying that your depression feels sort of like a thick fog, and that's why you can't concentrate? Or is it that you feel spaced out and unable to focus when you need to?" We will try our best to help you describe what you are going through. We do this to ensure that you have the correct diagnosis, and also to ensure that we fully understand your experience.

The fifth and final sign is that they periodically talk you through all you have accomplished, and make sure you agree. Now, I know that every therapist has their style and may not like to focus so much on goals and plans, but I believe that for us to benefit fully from therapy there need to be some objectives, and we need someone to check in on them regularly. This is not only pivotal in building a trusting and healthy therapeutic relationship, but it also increases our faith in the therapy process. Knowing that all our hard work is paying off and hearing from our ally how much we have grown keeps us motivated.

This check-in shouldn't be done all the time, but every few months or so is appropriate. I do this with my patients if I feel they are losing hope, or struggling with negative thoughts about themselves and their progress. I usually just open up their file and go back a few months, reminding them of that time and how well they managed everything that was going on. We all need to be reminded of our growth from time to time, and having a therapist who can do this when you may not even know you need it is an excellent sign that you have an amazing one.

There are so many more signs and stories I could share about good and bad therapists, but the most important component is that you like them and feel okay talking with them about all that's going on. I know it can be hard to figure out whether or not we like someone when the therapeutic relationship is so different, and that's why we will jump into that next. Let's figure out what a healthy relationship with a therapist looks like, and how we can know if we really click with them or not.

chapter 7

Is My Therapist a Good Fit?

Feeling the "Click" in a Therapeutic Relationship

Much of the research supporting the validity of therapy is contingent upon the connection we have with our therapist. To feel brave enough to work through what's haunting us, we need to like them and feel safe with them. But this relationship everyone talks about isn't easily explained or understood. Many people believe it needs to feel like a friendship, while others don't think they need to be emotionally connected to the therapist at all. The truth is, it's somewhere in between those two extremes.

Therapy is a professional, treatment-oriented relationship, so treating time in counseling as though you were having coffee with a friend will inevitably leave you still needing help. On the flip side, not feeling connected to the therapist at all can make it hard to open up. If they don't listen to us and show signs that they care, we can shut down or lose interest in going back.

That's why the ideal therapeutic relationship seems hard to pin down, but I promise you that it's a pretty easy thing to figure out. While everyone is going to have different expectations, things they look for, and what makes them comfortable, there are some fundamental ways to know if your therapist is a good fit for you.

We all get nervous before starting therapy, but when we get there we should feel that the process is more relaxed or more comfortable than we expected. We may not even know why, but we like them, and the questions they ask make talking about hard things a bit easier. I have heard from a lot of my viewers that when they found the right therapist, they finally felt therapy could work. All the nerves we may have had leading up to a session fall away, and we can express why we sought treatment in the first place.

It will also feel like they "get" you. I know that's not a clinical term, but there's no better way to describe the feeling. When you are telling them about experiences you have had or how a certain relationship made you feel, they can follow along easily. There's no need for much clarification, or asking what caused you to respond that way; they understand you and your process.

Having someone easily understand our situation and process can be validating. Fears that we have overreacted or that everything going wrong in our life is entirely our fault are the main reasons people are afraid to start therapy. A good friend of mine has refused to get into therapy for years because of this.

I know you say therapy helps people, but I have too much going on to make time for that. What if I get there and finally start sharing how I feel only to hear that I am overreacting? Or worse, that it's all my fault? I would completely come undone!

When we speak up and share our story, having the therapist nod along and understand can make all that irrational fear disappear. Also, just in case you're worried, a mental health professional should never tell you that something is all your fault. Situations in life are not black and white, and a proper therapist would avoid all-or-nothing statements, instead helping us see our role as well as how others may have influenced the situation. Being blamed for something not going right isn't going to make anyone feel good or want to open up more, so know that it has no place in the therapeutic setting.

Whether we want to acknowledge it or not, we all have age and gender preferences when it comes to picking a therapist. Many people who have survived abuse in their life will prefer to see a therapist of the opposite sex as their abuser. This can help them to feel safe in session, as well as more comfortable talking about the abuse they survived. Others will want to see an older therapist because they think they are wiser or better trained.

I prefer to see an older female therapist who is a bit on the hippie side. I haven't thought about why, but it's probably because I still feel very young in many ways and want to hear from someone who's already been where I am. I also love a different perspective, and I don't want anyone too stuffy or serious. That can cause me to swing into my type-A persona, when I feel the urge to do everything perfectly, and that's not very therapeutic.

I also tend to feel that women are more in tune with emotions (I know this is completely sexist, but these are my preferences), and I am more comfortable crying and venting about my angst to a woman. Now would be a good time for you to consider who you would prefer to see. Set aside all urges to be politically correct, and focus on what's most comfortable for you. If you don't know what you prefer or have a hard time getting started, here are some fundamental questions:

1. Who do I usually talk to when I am having a hard time?

2. Are my closest friends and confidants a certain age or gender?

3. Would I be okay with talking to someone much younger than me? What if they were much older? Would that be better or worse?

4. What about someone who is the same gender?

5. Could I see someone who is the gender I am attracted to? Would that be uncomfortable?

You don't have to know why you feel the way you do when answering these questions. What's important is that you are honest with yourself. You are the one who is going to be participating in therapy, so we need to make sure you are entirely comfortable.

> We all have age and gender preferences when it comes to picking a therapist. Set aside all urges to be politically correct, and focus on what's most comfortable for you.

Another way to know if you have a good fit in therapy is by answering this question: do you trust them easily? The answer should be yes. The therapeutic relationship isn't like any other, so it should not take months to gain your trust. For one, due to patient confidentiality, they can't tell anyone anything that's said in your sessions together.

(Confidentiality is a requirement in therapy that keeps anything said in therapy private, with a few legal exceptions.) Secondly, they spent years in school learning to help people just like you. That means they want to see you do well and help in any way they can. When it's the right therapist for you, trust will be something you can give comfortably.

If you found yourself nodding along as I went through these points, then you have discovered a therapist who fits! While that is a great thing, we also need to consider just how connected we feel to them, because there is such a thing as too much.

What If I Feel Attached to My Therapist?

Attachment is something I talk about online every day. However, no one talks about it in my regular life. I assume this is because people either don't know what attachment means, or aren't sure what feelings are healthy or not. Also, there is a lot of shame and embarrassment connected to attachment in relationships, and no one wants to bring it up in person for fear that how they feel is somehow wrong or makes them look crazy.

Attachment is a deep emotional and physical bond that someone feels for another person.[1] This bond normally first appears as our connection to our primary caregivers, like our mom or dad; when we are born, we form a deep attachment to the person who feeds us and cares for us. This connection is hardwired into our brain and exists as a way to ensure we are safe and cared for when we need it most.

As we grow up this attachment can present in many if not all of our relationships. Have you ever had a friend who shares that they love their new significant other after only dating a week? Or maybe you have that acquaintance who never lets anyone get to know them and breaks up with people if they try. Those behaviors are symptoms of the attachment they developed when they were an infant.

Since this early connection to others seems to find its way into most of our relationships, of course this can be an issue in therapy. Although the therapeutic relationship is different from any other we have, that doesn't make it immune to our existing relationship struggles. In fact, because therapy can make us feel so trusting, safe, and comfortable, we may find that even if we can keep our emotional struggles under control in our regular life, they come out full force in therapy.

Just like the two examples I briefly touched on, attachment in therapy can either feel like we never want our therapist to leave or that we would prefer to leave them first to avoid personal upset. When we feel that we never want our therapist to go and fear it happening, we can act in ways we think will keep them around. For example:

> I hate to even put this out there publically, but I used to tell my therapist that I was doing worse whenever I felt she was talking about stopping or lessening our sessions. I just needed to see her, and I didn't know how else to tell her.

We can want them to stay around so badly that we may even hurt ourselves to get them to stay. That's why there is so much shame and embarrassment associated with attachment, and why we need to talk about it more. Wanting someone to stay doesn't make us wrong; it merely tells us that we didn't get our emotional needs met as a child. Once we understand where they come from we can feel more validated and hopeful about making those up-setting urges stop.

Where Does My Attachment Urge Come From?

Research narrows the period our attachment develops to our first four or five years of life. During this time we rely heavily on our primary caregiver (usually our mom or dad) for much of our care. When we cry they come to our aid, and when we are hungry they feed us. When we feel we can depend on them to meet our physical and emotional needs, we form a secure attachment and feel safe to go out into the world and connect with others.[2] Having this secure attachment means it's not likely that we will worry about our therapist leaving, or struggle with intimacy with others.

If when we were young no one came when we cried or our caregiver was not consistently there when we needed them, we might form an insecure attachment. Our parents not being there when we needed them sent the message that our needs were not essential, or possibly false. Many of my patients who grew up in these situations share how their mothers would tell them to be quiet and go back to their room, some even refusing to hold them when they asked.

I know a lot of this sounds harsh and you may be wondering how a mother or father could do this, but often it's because of other things going on. Perhaps another child in the family is suffering from a chronic or deadly illness, or the family is going through a difficult financial situation and both parents have to work full time. Whatever the reasons, when we don't know that a parent cares for us entirely, we may try to find someone who will. That's why attachment presents so strongly in therapy.

What If I Don't Feel Connected
to My Therapist?

Often those of us who didn't have a loving and supportive environment growing up can struggle to let anyone near us. When a child's caretaker isn't around when the child cries for them, they sometimes stop crying or reaching out for help. In a way, they see their efforts as a waste and give up; therefore, instead of the above scenario, where we want to be closer to our therapist and see them more often, many patients have a hard time connecting at all.

Struggling to let people in can make therapy tricky because if it doesn't feel safe to let someone close to us emotionally, our therapist won't have enough information to help us. I get questions all the time from people about how to best open up; often they do not even understand what is holding them back. I want you to know that feeling like this is not your fault, and there are many tips and tools we can use to help you overcome these urges and benefit from treatment.

I always recommend journaling, but in this case it's imperative to start journaling. I know it's hard and you may not know what to write down, but just start! Here are some simple prompts:

- What happened today? Was any of it exciting? Frustrating?

- Did you feel overwhelmed today? Or possibly bored?

- Who did you see today? Do you like them? Why or why not?

- How do you feel now that your day is finished?

- What do you hope for tomorrow?

I know journaling can just seem like an adult term for keeping a diary, but trust me, it helps. As we start keeping track of our days, how we feel, and what's upsetting us, we can bring that information into therapy. Naturally, this will all happen as you feel open and okay with it, but it gives your therapist a way to connect with you. Then when your therapist reads it and validates your experience, you can begin to slowly let them get closer.

Building off of journaling, make sure you know you can start with small bits of information. I know I told you I just blurt everything out in my therapy sessions, but that doesn't work for everyone. You can start by sharing things that don't feel too scary or embarrassing. By giving your therapist the opportunity to listen and support you while you share, you are allowing yourself to be open to this relationship being different. In a way, we are teaching ourselves that it's okay to let people in sometimes.

Also, know that you can talk to your therapist about your issues with opening up. If we can't talk about the things that have been bothering us from our past, we can at least talk about what's going on right now. It's an odd thing to go into an appointment with a virtual stranger and talk about our deepest and darkest secrets, so know that therapists deal with this all the time. This conversation can be a bridge to building trust in other areas, and again it gives our therapist the opportunity to show us how reliable and caring they are.

Another technique to shortcut the struggle to open up is to begin by naming the emotions surrounding it. If we aren't okay talking about a trauma we experienced, we can instead say something like "I just feel anxious about sharing." Even identifying the emotion we encounter because of it can help! I know that coming up with what we feel can be difficult enough sometimes, so using a feelings chart can be another great help. (A feelings chart is simply a list of emotions. You can find them online and use them to help identify how you are feeling in the moment.)

How Can We Better Manage Our Attachment?

If we find ourselves wanting to talk to our therapist all the time, wanting to see them with more frequency, and continuously pushing the boundaries they set, we are going to have to speak to them about it. I know we often worry that this will drive them away:

> I understand that a therapeutic relationship is unequal
> in nature, but sometimes I wish my therapist shared
> more about herself. I sometimes feel that she's unsure
> about how to manage my strong attachment feelings
> toward her. I really feel connected to her as my therapist,
> and I don't want this relationship to end anytime soon.
> But I'm concerned that if I keep voicing my attachment
> issues toward her, she might consider referring me out to
> another therapist. I don't know what to do.

The truth is that it's all about the way we approach it with them. I know that many therapists out there may be upset that I am sharing this information, but it is most helpful if you stay with your current therapist to work through your attachment issues. Being able to work it through with the one you are attached to can help keep you from piling on another experience of abandonment or trauma.

If we tell a therapist that we feel close to them and want to know more about them, or even try to call them in between sessions when it's not an emergency, they may think we need a higher level of care. Many may try to reassert the boundaries of therapy, and this can feel like they are ignoring you or pulling away. Instead of taking action to get closer and closer to your therapist, when that's not what therapy's about, try talking about where you think it's coming from. Here is how I would phrase this struggle to your therapist:

> You know how I've been telling you how I feel connected and attached to you? It has been bothering me, and I was hoping we could figure out where that's coming from so I can stop feeling like this.

By focusing on where the urges to connect with your therapist come from, the strain they may have put on your therapeutic relationship can be lessened. This can also help guide your therapist toward your next treatment goal. Most therapists will know what is causing them, but in case they don't, by approaching it this way you are guiding them in the right direction. And, yes, I know it sounds odd that we should have to escort our therapists, but they can only help us if they have all the information. By telling them you think these urges are stemming from something in your past, they can help you look into it and work through it.

Attachment and Trauma

Attachment can often come from traumatic experiences because if we are a baby and nobody's there when we need them, it can be horrifying. We may worry that no one will ever come to help us, or whether we are wanted at all. These feelings can be very sensitive and leave us feeling even more vulnerable, so make sure you go at your own pace in therapy. There is never any pressure to hurry or talk about it all at once.

I know that being upset over not having someone there when we were an infant can seem silly or as if we are overreacting, but I promise we are not. The thing that's most difficult for my patients is to understand that they could have been terrified when no one came to hold them. If we consider how quickly children get upset, imagine not being able to take care of yourself and that no one cares for you no matter what you do; you can see how frightening that may have been. But because we don't form long-term memory until we are around five years old, it's hard for us to know how we felt at that time. Many of my patients will try to downplay what happened and how they felt because as an adult it can seem silly; but to that child it was terrifying.

Instead of allowing yourself to focus on why it shouldn't have affected you as much as it did, work on accepting how you feel. I know it is easier said than done, but something that has helped many of my patients is writing letters to their younger self. Focusing on that can be a great way to express how upset you may feel and how you wish you could have done more to make it stop. It can also be great to connect emotionally to your younger self. When we go through any trauma as a child, we can shut off our emotions as a way to push through and survive. Connecting through writing gives us the opportunity to begin to feel all the things we couldn't back then. Since I know this can be hard to conceptualize, here's an example:

Dear Baby Samantha,

I know that we haven't talked like this before, and in all honesty, I have tried to forget that you ever existed. I am so sorry about that. It has just been too painful for me to think about, and I hoped that pretending nothing ever happened would mean it wouldn't bother me anymore. But here I am, writing to you. First, I just want to say that I know how scared you are, and how unfair everything seems, but you will be okay. It gets awful for a while when Mom starts dating that guy with the big tattoo on his arm, but don't worry, she figures out how much he's hurting us, and she makes him leave. I wish there was more we could have done then; I remember screaming for Mom for hours until I finally gave up. I am sure you are angry and are getting into fights at school. Please try to talk to someone. I always wish I had done something to get us help sooner! Ugh! I know now that people are there to help, so realize that you won't feel like this forever. I know it will get better.

Love,

Adult Samantha

Writing these letters may be an exercise that you complete over and over, almost like your younger self is your pen pal. As you get more and more comfortable with it, you may be able to go into more detail, or other memories may crop up. Think of this as a creative therapeutic exercise and let it take you wherever you need. By doing this we can uncover repressed memories and begin to heal from all that happened when we were young.

What If I Have a Crush on My Therapist?

You may have thought you were the only one who ever had romantic feelings for your therapist, but it is very common. Just as lack of care and love in childhood can cause us to attach to our therapist, it can also cause us to want to date them. The psychological term we use for this is *erotic transference,* which means we are transferring onto our therapist some issues with love and relationships from our past.

I describe it as "issues with love and relationships" because this type of urge does not usually come from a romantic place. Instead, it develops as a result of not being shown proper love as a child. If we grew up knowing that when someone loved us, they were there, listening, caring, and supporting, then we can healthfully show love to others later in life. We know what it looks like and we understand that love can look and feel differently depending on who it's directed toward.

However, if no one was really there emotionally for us to demonstrate platonic versus romantic love, or even that people can be caring toward others, we may get confused. Since a therapist can be kind, patient, and attentive it can trigger feelings of love, and we may not know what they mean. Also, we don't know that much about our therapist, and our mind can fill in the blanks as it wants, creating a fantasy person that may be very different from who our therapist really is.

The good news is that this is very common, and can be worked through in therapy. While it may be hard even to consider bringing this up in session, it's the best thing you can do. Expressing what has come up for you can be a turning point in your treatment, and help guide your sessions through a more in-depth conversation about your past. While I can't promise that your therapist will understand and work with you on your history right away, I hope they at least try to figure out where these romantic feelings could be coming from. Naturally, before sharing any of this with them make sure they are good at their job, and if not, stop seeing them immediately.

Just so there isn't any misunderstanding, I want to emphasize that your therapist should never respond by saying they have feelings for you too. I know that if you have a crush or think you're in love with your therapist, this could be upsetting, but it is illegal for them to respond in kind. It's not illegal because anyone wants to tell you who you can and cannot date; it's against the law for the patient's safety.

Therapy is such a one-sided relationship, as we have discussed, and therefore puts the patient at a disadvantage. Meaning that you don't know where your therapist lives, what they like to do, what they struggle with, or who they are. They know all of that about you, and you see them as a professional. Without realizing it, we can give our therapists too much power, and if they abuse that, it could be dangerous.

Every state has a law against this for any mental health profession; the only difference is how many years after termination of the therapeutic relationship the prohibition lasts. Even if we stop seeing our therapist with the hope that we would then be able to date them, the law forbids it, and they could lose their license. In some states it's three years, in others it's five, but regardless, it's not something I support happening no matter how many years have passed.

How Can I Trust Therapy Again?

Picking someone who can sit with you while you dig through your troubles is an important decision, and you shouldn't feel rushed to make it. So take your time, and see a few therapists before you decide which one is right for you. I know this sounds cheesy and nonscientific, but you will feel it in your gut when it's right.

I know many of us worry whether our "gut" is even working, because it has led us down the wrong path in the past. I have heard from numerous viewers that the thought of getting back into therapy after a bad experience is terrifying, and many refuse to consider it again. While I will never dispute that some people are terrible at their jobs, it's also true that there are many amazing therapists out there. Therefore, I believe it's worth taking another chance given all you now know.

First, I want you to know that it's not your fault. When we are seeking therapy, it can be hard not to believe that mental health professionals know everything and are going to help us fix whatever's wrong. Communication about what therapy can be is the responsibility of the therapist, not you. If they didn't know how to help you with your specific issue or didn't think it was a good fit, it was up to them to talk with you about it and refer you to someone else. Don't let negative thoughts fill your mind, and instead remember that therapy involves two people, and the one you pay is supposed to be trained to ensure it's helpful.

Second, take your time choosing who you want to work with next. I know that when we finally make an appointment to see someone, we want to be done with searching and to start feeling better, but don't rush. Now is the time to consider what you are looking for in a therapist; check to make sure they are demonstrating all the signs of a good therapist and you feel that "click" with them. If there are any red flags, or if you ever feel they aren't taking you seriously, bring it up with them. A competent professional will be able to talk you through it and hopefully assure you that they are on your side working with you. If they don't, it's okay to move on.

Last, once you have found another clinician to work with, talk through that previous experience. Talking this through with someone who is good at their job can help us heal, and help us regain our trust in the therapeutic process. It can take time, and you may go through periods of questioning their dedication, but having that be part of your work together can ensure you always feel supported.

Therapy Isn't Perfect

If you happen to be type A or maybe you just enjoy pleasing others, therapy can be painful to participate in without feeling like you have to do everything perfectly. I have had many patients who always complete their homework, are on time for all appointments, and regularly let me know how much they feel therapy is helping them. Of course, this makes me feel good and like that I am helping them feel better, but if this continues for very long, I become suspicious. Not because I think they are lying, but because I wonder if they know it's okay to have a hard time and show their imperfect side in therapy.

It can be hard for us to let people see us at our worst, or to talk about a time when we let someone down. But that's what therapy's for! It's the one place where we can shout, cry, and be our worst self without being judged or ridiculed. I can honestly say that this is a lesson that was hard for me to learn. I didn't want to let my first therapist down, or disappoint her, so I tried to do everything she asked, just as she asked it. In the end, I never got the help I needed.

When I began college and started seeing a new therapist, she saw my people-pleasing, type-A baggage from a mile away. As a result, one of her first assignments for me was to be unreachable for a whole day, and to only do whatever I wanted to do. I couldn't do it. I was so upset with myself and my inability to do what was asked of me that I went back to therapy, head down, and told her. To my surprise, she wasn't upset but rather excited that she was on the right track; she had correctly identified one of my issues, and knew what we should work on next.

That was the beginning of therapy for me. I could finally let my guard down, knowing that I wasn't going to disappoint her, and I was able to unpack the reason I sought outside approval so much. This scenario doesn't mean that my first therapist was terrible at her job, but that she wasn't the right fit for me. I needed to know that therapy could be messy, and outside the lines, for it to benefit me. Finding someone who pushed me to figure out why I worked so hard to please others was critical to my healing.

If you find yourself wanting to please your therapist or do everything they suggest, make sure you bring it up. Talk about how it feels, and why you have probably done this sort of thing for most of your life; trust me, you will discover so much about yourself that you have kept hidden all these years. That's the magical side of therapy, and why finding the right therapist can make all the difference.

chapter 8

What Are Toxic Relationships?

Warning Signs and Ways to Get Out of Them

Maybe it's just me, but the phrase "toxic relationship" seems to be used more frequently lately. I have no idea who or what started this trend, but I do have some personal and professional experience with these types of relationships that I would like to share. I do not believe people themselves are toxic; however, certain behavior and relationships can be. One of my favorite quotes, which describes my beliefs about this, comes from my friend and fellow YouTube videos creator Cat Valdes:

> One person isn't completely responsible for a bad relationship; sometimes it's just a bad recipe.

I love what Cat says because it's the truth. With all the other options available, why even bother with a combination we are pretty sure won't work out? We can say the same thing about any relationships we create in life, whether they are platonic or romantic.

A toxic relationship isn't always as easy to recognize as two ingredients that don't mix well together. It can feel good at first, sometimes comfortable, and in many cases it may feel like the best relationship we have had in a long time. However, slowly but surely it can feel like every button we have is being pushed, and we don't even recognize ourselves or how we are acting when we are together. While each unhealthy situation can feel unique to those in it, there are five types of toxic relationships therapists see over and over again. The more we can learn about them, and know what signs to look for, the more easily we can avoid them.

Enmeshment—Lack of Independence

This kind of connection can be intoxicating, and move so quickly that after a few weeks we can't seem to imagine our life without this person in it. There are no boundaries in place, no time apart. We may even look to them to help us make any and all decisions in our life. While wanting someone around and enjoying the time together are completely fine, needing someone there all the time is not. I know that may feel like an insignificant differentiation to make, but trust me, it's quite essential.

I had a boyfriend in between college and graduate school who was extremely dependent, but I didn't realize it right away. It started out as a pretty typical relationship, with us going on dates on the weekend while leaving the weekdays for work and time with friends. However, it slowly became more and more enmeshed and unhealthy. He began texting me to ask where I was anytime we weren't together, even needing me to help him plan out his schedule and pick a graduate school. It seemed that I was the only person in the relationship who was capable of making any decisions. I quickly became tired of all the pressure and planned to talk to him about it, and possibly end the relationship.

We were sitting in his apartment when I knew exactly how I was going to figure out if he was utterly dependent on me or not. I asked him, "Do you want me around all the time, or do you need me around?" Without hesitation, he emphatically stated, "I *need* you around, of course!" It was then I knew we had to break up. I know that might sound dramatic, but it's much healthier to be wanted, not needed. I felt his need, and it weighed on me and our relationship. I was exhausted and easily irritated by him. I had to know if this was a personal issue I needed to work on, or if it was us as a couple that wasn't working. His answer told me it was us; we were a bad recipe.

When a relationship becomes based on need instead of want, it's no longer enjoyable. Just consider things you want to do versus those you need to do. They are very different, right? Need signifies that someone cannot manage without you, and if we honestly think about it, we *can* live without someone else. We were existing before we met them. The problem is that the media as a whole supports this toxic style of a relationship in movies, television shows, and songs. Country music is the worst; one of my all-time favorite musicians, Tim McGraw, even has a song titled "I Need You."

The critical component to recognizing each of these toxic styles is the red flags to look out for so we can avoid them much more easily. With an enmeshed or dependent relationship, the most significant red flag is our ability to do things by ourselves. Is it okay to go out with other friends or do something on your own? Does your partner or friend give you a hard time when you do? Notice how you feel when you choose to be independent and do things solo. If you feel guilty or awful about it, then you may want to speak up, address the concern, and possibly make some changes to the relationship to create more balance.

Another red flag is decision making. If decisions that in no way affect the other person feel impossible for you to make on your own, that's a sign the relationship isn't healthy. Sure, we can ask for advice when we need it, but not being able to act on our own shows how much of our self-worth and identity are tied up in the relationship.

Just remember that there are two people in every relationship, and when it comes to dependency, you are both guilty. That's why we have to be open to talking about it, recognizing our part in the issue, and working to make it better. Just because we find our relationship falls under this category doesn't mean it's doomed; it shows us that we need to focus more on ourselves and our self-care. As long as both of you are working to make it better, it will get there.

The Master Manipulator

Unlike the first style, this one usually involves only one member of the partnership. The tough thing about manipulation is that the victims don't notice it right away. Master manipulators usually wait until we are comfortable and connected to them before they begin their harmful behavior. Even those who are manipulating us may not realize they are doing it. I find people who exploit others are often too preoccupied with their own emotions and interests to be aware of how their actions affect someone else.

Obviously, this toxic style can play out in various ways, but I am going to focus my thoughts and advice on those who manipulate others to get them to stay and those who use other people for their advancement. Both are unhealthy and detrimental to the victim, but the reasoning behind each is very different.

The main difference is that when someone tries to get you to stay in a relationship with them, they are doing it because they were hurt before. Those who manipulate us to stay don't even know they are doing it; it's more of a coping or defense mechanism. On the other hand, when we are using someone to advance our agenda, we are entirely self-serving and are not acting out of our pain. It is done maliciously with nothing but our own goals in mind.

When thinking about manipulation occurring as a way to ensure someone stays in our life, I automatically recall my friend Bobby's first real relationship. He was sixteen and in high school, and therefore very naive. He and his girlfriend dated for about four or five months before Bobby decided it wasn't going to work out. He was the life of the party, while she didn't like being social at all. They would get into fights every weekend because she wanted to stay in and watch movies, and Bobby wanted to go hang out with his friends. After a while he just didn't feel like he could put up with it anymore, and one weekend he decided to break up with her.

He was supposed to meet up with the rest of us after the basketball game (and breakup) to tell us how it went, but he never showed up. When we all got back to school the following Monday, Bobby and his girlfriend were still holding hands. We were shocked! Bobby later explained that he did in fact try to break up with her, but she wouldn't let him. We all thought he was crazy, or at least not telling us the full truth. There just wasn't any way he would still be dating her if he had already tried to break up with her, right? Well, as it turns out, we were wrong.

He later shared that when he tried to break up with her, she started crying and refused to let him go. She begged him to stay, and after talking for over two hours, he wasn't even sure what they were talking about anymore. He got up to leave, telling her it just wasn't going to work out because they were too different. That's when she threatened to kill herself.

Remember, we were only sixteen years old, and this was his first serious relationship. He didn't know what to do, so he told her he would stay and they could still be together. That lasted for about a month or two, but she did manipulate him to get him to stay.

I share that story because as a result of my years working in treatment centers and hospitals, I realized manipulation is much more common than I had thought. I know you may assume that anyone who would try to trick someone into staying with them must be desperate or hate being alone, but it's so much more than that.

The reasons behind why someone would trick you into staying rather than be alone have to do with trauma and self-worth. First, as I said previously, trauma in childhood can create an unhealthy attachment style that can leave us searching for a proper caregiver. We may easily attach to people we haven't known for very long; not having anyone there for us feels too scary to manage. Some of my patients have even reported that feeling lonely is in some ways retraumatizing to them.

If a caregiver failed to stop a trauma, or didn't believe us when we told them what was happening, we might have decided that our feelings and thoughts were not valid. Therefore, we now don't feel safe or whole when we are alone. Keeping someone around to protect us and emotionally support us becomes the most vital goal in our life, and we may take extreme measures to ensure we are never left alone.

Then there is lack of self-worth. When we don't feel good about who we are or believe we are worthwhile, we can rely on our relationships for it, seeking out someone who can be and do what we aren't able to be and do for ourselves. This could be as simple as finding someone who is confident and self-assured, or someone who is nurturing and loving.

Even though needing someone else to validate our worth isn't healthy, it is a survival technique. Not having the confidence necessary to live a successful life and have a healthy view of ourselves could have held us back and caused us to be hurt even more. By finding someone who can support us when we need it, we have a better sense of security and can take on life's challenges as they come.

Self-worth was the cause in my friend Bobby's case. His girlfriend was an identical twin who always felt unfavorably compared to her sister. Her sister seemed to excel at everything, getting straight As, being the first chair in band, and making the varsity soccer team her freshman year. As a result, her parents seemed to give her sister more attention and praise; Bobby's girlfriend never felt that she mattered. So she found Bobby and relied on him for the validation and emotional support she never got as a child, and ended up wearing him out.

That's the problem with depending on another person for our self-worth: they can't make us love ourselves. Even with words of affirmation and support, they can't change what we believe; that has to come from inside. That's why our self-talk is vital to our overall mental health. It can push us into unhealthy relationships and ruin any healthy ones we may have.

Red flags concerning this type of toxic relationship can vary from person to person, but the biggest one is words of affirmation.

If someone looks to you to make them feel good about themselves, possibly not even believing you when you tell them how amazing they are, notice how often it occurs. If this is happening all the time, it's best to try and talk with them about it so you can better understand why. If it's more than you can give or manage, then it's probably best to end the relationship before it completely wears you out.

Last, notice if they connect their value to being with you. One of my friends used to have an insecure boyfriend who insisted on her getting dressed up every time they went out. He would then comment about how attractive a couple she made them, and how everyone was probably jealous of him. While that's quite the compliment, it always sounded to me like he didn't feel right about who he was unless she was there, and that's not something we want in a relationship.

Moving into the more deceitful type of manipulation, recognizing those who do it for personal gain is a bit more cut and dried than the previous style. They are usually seeking money or power. If you find yourself in a position of having more of either of these things, be cautious. This doesn't mean it's not safe to trust anyone; it just means that if we have more money or power than someone we are in a relationship with, we need to assess whether or not they could be in it only for that.

I am not going to try and explain away completely self-serving and exploitive behavior. People who see others as things to be used and rather than valued have no place in my book or in my mind. They are terrible human beings, and we need to know how to protect ourselves against them.

Since I said we need to assess whether a person could be using us, let me define what I mean by that. If someone is going to try and use us, they will seek us out first. This could start off casually, like making a new friend at the office, but they won't wait long before asking you for a favor. It will usually be something small at first; they do it to see how willing you are, as well as how much you have of what they want.

If this is getting a bit obscure, consider this example:

It's so hard for me to look back on my relationship with Julie because I don't know what was real or not. She was so nice at first, and we became fast friends. Going out for lunch almost every day, and our happy hour tradition on Fridays. She was the first friend I truly made at work. Then her life just seemed to fall out from underneath her. Her mom got terribly ill, and Julie had to send all her money back home. Then she got kicked out of her apartment because she was late on her rent, and her boyfriend left her. Before I knew it, she was living with me, and I was pretty much supporting her financially. It wasn't until my brother came to visit that I saw what she was doing. When I tried to bring it up she was extremely defensive, we got into a huge fight, and she took her stuff and left. I haven't talked to her since. My brother still pressures me to sue her for the over $4,000 she owes me, but I can't bring myself to. I just miss my friend, or who I thought was my friend.

Hopefully, that gives you a better idea of how this type of manipulation can occur. Another red flag is how quickly they want things to progress once you know each other fairly well. In the example above, Julie didn't waste much time before sharing some life drama and asking to move in. Take your time in relationships, and know that if you feel something is moving too fast, or someone is asking too much, it's entirely okay to say no or to ask for some time to think about it.

Finally, ask your tried and true friends or family for their opinion. So many times those closest to us hold back their real thoughts about a relationship we are in so they don't hurt us. Asking them to share their real feelings can help you better gauge whether you have every reason to be suspicious of this person, or if you are overreacting.

Abusive Relationships

Many people automatically assume they would never find themselves in an abusive relationship. Even my friends will say things like "If a man ever tried to lay a hand on me, that would be it! I would never allow someone to treat me that way." We all have our own beliefs about what abuse looks like and what it would mean if we found ourselves in a relationship like that. The truth is, abuse isn't always so easy to notice, and it happens with more frequency than we realize.

The two types of abuse I want to focus on are physical and emotional. Regardless of what you think or have been told, both forms of abuse are dangerous and damaging. The struggle many of my viewers and patients face is the stigma they feel for having been or currently being in an abusive relationship; it is terrible and often prevents them from telling anyone.

The stigma I am talking about is any of those automatic thoughts you have about abuse. Like I stated above, many of my friends proudly declare they would never find themselves in that situation. So what does that say to someone who was or is in a relationship like that? That they are weaker? Or more stupid? Consider what thoughts came up for you when you first read this section's title, and be aware of them before talking to anyone dealing with an abusive relationship.

Before getting into what the cycle of abuse is, know that it is never okay for someone to harm you physically. It doesn't matter if you were talking back, being rude, or even screaming at them. Nothing we do should ever warrant physical harm; it's the abuser's actions that are to blame, not yours. This goes for emotional abuse as well. Being regularly put down, blamed for anything that goes wrong, or controlled in any way is not part of a healthy relationship, and you don't have to put up with it.

Abuse occurs in relationships for many reasons. Some blame it on abuse the abusers themselves sustained when they were younger, while others say it's a personality disorder. Whatever the cause, the reason we struggle to get out of a relationship like that is the cycle of abuse, a theory originally termed the cycle of violence, developed by Lenore E. Walker to describe the patterns she found in abusive relationships.[1] However, because not all abuse is violent or physically harmful, it is now called the cycle of abuse.

There are four stages in this cycle, and I think it's important to understand what each stage can look and feel like. That way you will be better able to recognize if this is something going on in your relationship because as I said, not all abuse is quickly noticed and it's much more common than we think.

The first stage is called *tension building*, when small daily disagreements seem to escalate slowly. From arguing about why the house is so dirty, to who forgot to pick up the milk. The abuser can feel wronged, irritated, or disrespected and begin some abusive behaviors. In this stage most people being abused will report feeling like they are walking on eggshells; they try their hardest to keep their abuser happy so they won't get hurt. This can last for a few hours up to many months, but it will inevitably get worse and escalate to the next stage.

Stage two is called the *crisis phase*. This is when the abuse it-self takes place, and although small abusive situations could have already been occurring during the tension building phase, this is when it's at its worst. Whatever type of abuse regularly happens in this relationship, it occurs during this time.

The next two stages are why it can be so hard to get out of a toxic relationship like this, and why many stay in these situations for years. The third stage is called the *honeymoon* or *reconcilia-tion stage*. This is when the abuser apologizes for what they did; they may even buy gifts or swear it will never happen again. Some will even go so far as to threaten to harm themselves as a way to make up for what they did, and also to generate sympathy for themselves.

This can be incredibly confusing for the victim because the abuser can enter this stage immediately following the abuse, and while the perpetrator doesn't usually say anything about the abuse while it's happening, they may quickly become re-morseful. This may leave their partner wondering if maybe the abuser can change, that they didn't mean to do it after all. Many of my patients share that they wanted to believe their abuser and thought maybe if they were a better friend, daughter, or partner, it wouldn't happen again.

The final stage is called *calm;* this is when things go back to a regular relationship. The abuser may even offer to get into ther-apy, all the while continuing to apologize for what they did. As the abuse continues, many report that this stage goes away alto-gether; but it's important to know it can exist, and even if there are periods of normalcy, that doesn't in any way make up for the terror an abusive person has caused.

I hope that outlining these stages has helped you better un-derstand why people find themselves in abusive relationships.

It's also important to note that the abuse usually builds over time, and what may start out as passionate fights can turn into violence if left unaddressed. The good news in all of this is that there are some standard red flags we can look out for to help keep us far away from this type of toxic relationship.

The first red flag is if they seem always to expect you to check in, and want to know where you are at all times. I know this may seem sweet and caring at first, but we all need some space and freedom, and all healthy relationships are built on a level of trust. Make sure there is trust on both sides of any relationship you allow yourself to get into.

Second, does your partner always find ways to put you down? They could do this while you are out with friends or in private. However, if they tease us or use personal information to embarrass us in front of others, know that it's not okay and you deserve better.

Third, do they lose their temper quickly and over things that shouldn't be so upsetting? This can lead to the tension-building phase because if they are easily upset, we may try our best to keep everything just right so they don't explode. Yes, couples and friends will have fights from time to time, but you shouldn't feel that you regularly have to consider everything you do so you don't agitate them.

The last red flag, although there are many more signs specific to each type of abusive relationship, is isolation. If someone you are in a relationship with doesn't want you hanging out with others, or requires that you ask for permission before you go anywhere, that's abuse. This might manifest as checking your phone and texts, not allowing you to have a car, or even moving you away from everyone you are connected to. There are many ways someone can isolate us from those we care about, so if you begin to feel it's harder and harder to spend time with others, you may want to consider talking to a therapist or getting out of the relationship altogether.

The Black Hole

This next type of toxic relationship is one I am sure we are all very familiar with, and it is also usually created by one person. I call it the black hole because whatever excitement or energy we have is wholly devoured by them, and we are left with nothing. You may have heard these people described as emotional vampires, sucking from you every ounce of support and love you can muster. Whatever we decide to call it, these relationships cannot sustain themselves and are entirely toxic.

I had a friend for many years who only called me when she needed something. I dreaded her calls or texts because I knew it was going to cost me more than I wanted to give. Meaning that the amount of energy I had to give to our relationship was long gone, I was running on fumes, and I was beginning to resent her. I struggled to cut ties with her because we had known each other for so long, and I knew I was her only close friend.

Looking back, that should have been the first sign. So please learn from my mistakes; if you encounter someone who seems to have no close friends or they're always having issues with the ones they have, don't engage. Trust me; this will save you so much time and energy that would be better spent elsewhere.

Luckily, I do get smarter as I get older. When I brought up my issues with her in session, my therapist asked what I got out of the relationship. I can honestly (and sadly) say that I hadn't even considered that before. After a long silence, I said I wasn't sure. I hadn't been able to reach her when I was in crisis for many years, and every time we spoke she always turned the conversation to herself and how her problems were so much worse. Then my therapist mentioned something I will never forget:

Kati, healthy relationships are like a checking account. You both have to deposit love, trust, and support into it regularly to be able to take anything out. If you haven't made any deposits, you cannot expect to make a withdrawal.

If I was honest with myself, I had been the only one making deposits into our relationship account for as long as I could remember. I decided then and there that I was only going to match the deposits she made into our relationship. If she took the time to call and check in, and listen, I would do the same.

Just as my therapist and I had suspected, I no longer had to put any energy into it. She never called or asked how I was doing, so I didn't either, and over the past few years our relationship has died. Now, just because it was a toxic relationship doesn't mean it wasn't upsetting to let go or that I don't miss her. There was a reason we were friends for all those years, but that reason no longer exists, and if I'm honest, I had to take some time and grieve the loss.

After about a year of not having much contact, I can honestly say that I feel so much better. The stress and guilt I allowed myself to experience in the relationship were exhausting. Without that toxicity in my life, I am now able to put energy into people who are balanced and healthy, and even build some relationships. Yes, ending relationships can be hard, but when they are toxic the relief you feel is entirely worth it.

Just like all other forms of toxic relationships this one also has some red flags. So take notes, and don't make the same mistakes I did. The first warning sign is dreading your friend's calls or texts. If the thought of having to talk to them and be there for them is too exhausting to consider, you may want to think about engaging with them less. The second sign is feeling completely wiped out and exhausted after spending any time with them. We could feel this way after having dinner or even after a long phone call. If we leave every interaction feeling worse than when it started, it could help to examine what we are getting out of the relationship.

The final red flag is every conversation being all about them. We have all had those conversations when someone continually steers the topic back to themselves and how hard their life is. Again, it's hard to have any balance in a relationship when the focus is always on only one half of it. To test if this is indeed what's happening in your relationship, try starting off a conversation by telling them all about the crazy week you've had. If you can't make it through more than one situation in your week without their adding in something they went through, it's safe to say you've stumbled into a black hole.

The Green-Eyed Monster

The last type of relationship toxicity I frequently see is overwhelming jealousy. This can involve one or both members of the partnership and is found in both platonic and romantic situations. While it's entirely normal and healthy to experience jealousy from time to time, if we are overcome by it and act out of the feelings it generates, it can ruin our relationships.

When it comes to romantic relationships, jealousy is most often born out of insecurity. We may worry that the person we love will find someone better, cheat on us, or leave us. As you can see, all our concerns are based on our belief that we are not good enough, or don't measure up. This is why many mental health professionals believe we cannot healthfully love someone else if we don't first love ourselves.

The same can be said for our platonic relationships, because the only reason we would be jealous of someone would be that we don't feel we have enough, or are enough. I used to be jealous of so many of my classmates in college because unlike them, I didn't come from money. I went to Pepperdine University, an expensive private school in Southern California; everyone there seemed to have new cars, fancy clothes, and no concern whatsoever for the sheer cost of tuition. I, on the other hand, took out all my own loans, fought for as many scholarships as I could, and worked part time. I was jealous because what they had seemed so much more comfortable and effortless.

Again, my jealousy had nothing to do with my classmates or anything they did to me. I was just unhappy with myself and what I didn't have. I was looking over at their green field of grass thinking it must be so beautiful, luxurious, and comfortable. Over time, I was able to see that money didn't make life any better; the only thing that would do that was being happy with what I already had in my life. I know it's a hard lesson to learn, but practicing gratitude for what we have can help change our perspective and ideally kill any jealousy we are feeling.

The red flags and signs I am going to talk about can be applied to both ourselves and our relationships. I say that because much of what happens when jealousy is present is hidden or spoken behind others' backs, so it may take us a while to realize it was there at all. That's why the first sign is that we want to trash-talk others all the time, or they are talking badly about us behind our backs.

Undoubtedly, it may take some time for us to know what they are doing behind our back, but if you find yourself wanting to talk negatively about someone, judging their situation or lifestyle, try exploring how you are feeling about your own situation. Hopefully, that will show you why you are feeling the way you are, and you can put your focus back on your own life and how you can make it more enjoyable. Back to an earlier exercise, writing down three to five things you are grateful for each day can help create an environment in which jealousy cannot survive.

The next red flag is that the relationship feels controlling. They want to know where we are and what we are doing at all times. They could even get angry at us for going out with other people when they aren't able to join us. Again, this could be something we find ourselves doing, or something being done to us. Either way, know that a healthy relationship thrives on the freedom for each person to grow and develop. If we stifle that freedom, it will slowly suffocate and die.

The final red flag is the struggle to be happy for each other. If we get a promotion at work, they get upset because we now make more than they do. If we have a great day, they can't help but be angry because their day was terrible. Whatever it is, anything we do only seems to make them feel worse. Again, you can see how this reflects back on the person who is jealous rather than on the one doing well.

> We all deserve to have relationships built on trust, love, and mutual respect. Give yourself the opportunity to cultivate them.

Continuing to be in a toxic relationship like this can rob us of our happiness and leave us in an angry and sad place. But if we do our best to not engage in jealous conversations, and focus on what we have to be grateful for, we can rid our mind of overwhelming jealousy. So take some time and notice what is being said and what you say about yourself and others; make sure it's positive and supportive.

Overcoming Toxic Relationships for Good

The truth is that we will all have toxic relationships in our lives from time to time. Even while writing this chapter, I had to pick and choose which stories of mine to share because there were so many. The good news is that we can all choose to learn and grow. This means taking note of when we find ourselves acting out of anger or jealousy. It also means paying attention to how free we feel to be ourselves in our relationships, or if one tends to wear us out.

Take some time to assess which of your relationships are toxic or not, as well as which of them you want to try and work on versus the ones you may need to walk away from. Throughout this process, I would encourage you to always consider your part in them. The most significant mistake we can make is to assume we aren't to blame for any of it. Whether our role was to enable their bad behavior or just getting into the relationship in the first place, whatever it is, we need to identify it. If we don't, we could leave a relationship only to start another that ends the same way. In each partnership, there are two people, and each plays their role. If we figure out what ours is, what's healthy or unhealthy about it, then we can work to change. We all deserve to have relationships built on trust, love, and mutual respect. Give yourself the opportunity to cultivate them.

If you are still questioning whether or not the relationship you are in is toxic, here's a quick quiz to help sort that out.

Are You in a Toxic Relationship?

1. Do you put off seeing them or responding to their texts and calls?

2. Do you feel worse after having spent time with them?

3. Have they ever threatened to hurt you physically or emotionally?

4. Do they discourage you from doing things on your own?

5. Have they asked to borrow money and not paid it back?

6. Do they ask you for a lot of favors?

7. Do you struggle to make decisions without them?

8. Have you found out they were talking badly about you behind your back?

9. Do you constantly feel like you are walking on eggshells when you're around them?

10. Do they repeatedly put you down?

If you answered yes to more than one of these questions, I would encourage you to consider ending the relationship. If it's safe to do so, try to communicate to the other person what you are feeling and what changes you are trying to make. If both members of a relationship want to work to make it better, we can overcome these toxic tendencies. However, it cannot be accomplished alone. So consider your safety as well as your sanity, and make the choices that support your growth.

chapter 9

Communication

The Key to a Happy, Healthy Life!

We all know how important communication is in life, and more specifically in our relationships. I can honestly say that many of my past relationships, romantic or platonic, have ended because of a lack of communication, or due to miscommunication. Everyone is always reminding us that relationships are built on trust, but I would argue that it's communication that keeps our partnerships happy and healthy. In fact, we can't build confidence between ourselves and others if we don't openly express to them what they can expect, right? Therefore, I believe that trust cannot exist without explicit communication.

Before getting into how we can improve our communication skills, I think it's important to define the term. *Merriam-Webster's Collegiate Dictionary* defines communication as "a process by which information is exchanged between individuals through a common system of symbols, signs, or behavior." To me, this means that however we try to get our point across to someone, excluding mind reading, would be defined as communication. Keep this definition in mind as we walk through ways we can better connect with those around us.

Being told to just communicate better is overwhelming. Whenever we are working to change a long-term habit, it's going to take some time and patience. Many of us were raised to not talk about what we were feeling or what we were worried about. I can remember from a young age being protected from life's hard truths with the words "Everything is fine, now go in the back and play with your brother." This was said over and over whenever I heard my parents raising their voices and wanted to know what was going on.

Parents do this to protect their children. Many parents don't want their children to have to worry about or be upset by something they can't fully understand. The truth is that the more we talk with our children and give them the facts, the better off they will be. You see, communication not only allows a child to better understand what's going on, but also teaches them they can trust their feelings.

When we are told everything is fine, and we are pretty sure it's not, it can cause us to second-guess our gut response. If we hear raised voices and notice that our parents are angry, yet when we ask them what's wrong we are told, "Nothing," it can be confusing. In our mind we have all this evidence that our parents are upset and something is wrong; however, those we trust most in life are telling us everything is fine. Therefore, who in this situation must be mistaken? As children we usually feel it has to be us, and as a result we may struggle to trust ourselves to know what's okay and not okay, even when we have information to support what we feel.

I know that correlation seems extreme, and all parents keep things from their kids, but talking things out in an age-appropriate way is much healthier. Telling children that arguments happen, but you still love each other allows them not only to trust their feelings about a situation but also to know that disagreements are normal and okay.

Not being taught how to communicate about difficult things can lead us to struggle to develop healthy relationships and with-stand disagreements. We may find ourselves repeatedly in toxic situations or expecting those in our lives to be able to read our minds. Whatever the symptoms we experience, the good news is that we can learn new tools and methods to use when we want to fight or run away. Yes, these tips are going to be hard to integrate, but try to focus on one that seems doable, and be patient with yourself as you try it out. Remember, we have been communicating (healthfully or not) a certain way our whole lives; it is going to take more than a few days to change that.

Passive Aggression

To build on why most adults struggle to communicate with others, let's talk about passive aggression. If we are regularly told that how we feel isn't correct, and everything is always "fine," then as we age we may stop trying to speak up about how we feel at all. In truth, it has been quite a waste of time thus far, and therefore we put our energy elsewhere. Also, if we were raised in an abusive household, much of how we felt wasn't considered important anyway, and that could cause us to ignore our real emotions.

Again, I know that blaming our current issues on our past seems clichéd, but it's in our childhood that we learn how to express our needs and get them met. If no one is there or they choose to ignore us, it has a lasting effect. Which leads us to what causes so many people to act in a passive-aggressive way: their upbringing.

Aggression on its own is intense. It's what results when we let our emotions override our common sense: we fight with people. Aggression can cause anything from an NHL fight to war, and I think it's fair to say nothing positive has come out of acting aggressively. The difference between aggression and passive aggression is that one is easy to see while the other is elusive.

When someone is passive aggressive, they won't directly tell you how they feel. Even if you ask, they often don't know what to say, or will act like everything is fine. You can't expect a passive-aggressive person to let you know what you have done to upset them, or even how you can make it right. Instead, they will do small things to make your life difficult, such as make you late for that important meeting, or do all the laundry in the house but yours. When you ask them about it, they may deny it, or possibly not respond to you at all. Being around someone who acts this way can be very trying, and in many cases can lead to a toxic relationship.

The good news is that because we become passive aggressive when our feelings and thoughts are not taken into consideration, we can work to overcome our passive-aggressive urges. This means that if we start by identifying our feelings each day and then utilize the communication tips and tools in this chapter, we can stop upsetting ourselves and those around us, and ask for what we need.

Passive aggression happens when we don't know how, or don't feel able, to share how we feel. If we are upset by the way a friend treated us but lack the tools to express our feelings through direct communication, we can try to find other ways to let them know. Passive-aggressive solutions are usually indirect, and are detrimental to our relationships. Here's an example of how passive aggression can look:

> I was upset with my friend Lucy because she didn't make me her maid of honor. We had talked about this since we were in middle school, and I was so hurt that she picked Julie instead. I couldn't figure out how to tell her. She seemed so happy, which only made me more upset. As the dates of the bridal shower and bachelorette party got closer and closer, I only got angrier. So I decided at the last minute not to go and not to talk to her about it. She kept calling and wondering where I was, and I ignored her. If I'm honest, I was glad she was upset, because that's how I felt. At least she felt a little portion of the pain she put me through.

You can see how passive aggression doesn't accomplish anything positive and can kill a relationship. Unless we can figure out how we feel and express it to those we love, they aren't going to understand us or know how to stop the situation from happening again. That's why the only way to rid ourselves of passive-aggressive tendencies is to communicate. We must tell those in our lives about any upset, frustration, or hurt we feel, and be direct about it.

Directness doesn't imply aggression but instead states the issue to them in a transparent way. It can help to start journaling a bit about what has gone on and how you feel about it. That way we can give ourselves another chance to understand how we feel, and even practice how we would say it to those we care about. If you are particularly nervous, it can also be beneficial to imagine what the person might reply, and even be prepared for them to get upset. That way you can navigate all possible scenarios when you share with them how you are feeling.

I don't mean to make communication seem scary or overwhelming, because it isn't; it's pretty simple. But for those of you who dread talking directly to someone for fear of upsetting them or being misunderstood, the tips given in this chapter can be a big help in getting you started on the right foot. For the rest of you, consider how you feel, when the problem started, and what upset you. Without trying to blame someone else for how we feel (that would be passive aggressive and unhealthy), try expressing what you found upsetting. This will allow them to hear your side and give you the time to listen to them in return.

As with every change, it may be slow at first, and we may feel the urge to go back to our old, unhealthy ways, but keep trying. Instead of giving up and giving in, try to learn from the increase in the desire to act out. Consider these questions when struggling with the return of old habits:

- How have I been feeling lately? Relaxed? Stressed?

- Have I been taking care of myself? When did I last do something I enjoy?

- How have the past few days been? Did any conflict or small irritants occur?

- Have I been trying to express what I feel to those it affects?

- Have I been numbing out or ignoring my feelings?

Taking stock of how we feel and what's been going on can give us a better idea of what may have caused this struggle. Nothing in life happens in a vacuum, and if we can figure out what tends to trigger these urges, we can better prepare for or avoid them. For example, if we find ourselves reverting to passive-aggressive acts when stressed out, then maybe we have to increase our self-care during those times and take breaks. It can even help to use these questions as a check-in every few days. That can help any ignored upset to be acknowledged and dealt with before it turns into more.

Stick to the Facts

This tip is best when applied to a disagreement, or whenever we are asking for something we need. Sticking to the facts doesn't mean we should bombard another person with all the evidence we have or the things they have done to wrong us; it merely helps us keep our feelings and judgments out of it.

Sticking to the facts when we are in an argument allows us to communicate our view of what happened without getting caught up in how we felt about it. This means that if we got into a fight with a friend because she shared personal information we wanted kept private, we would say something like this:

> I am really upset because I thought that when I told
> you about my financial issues you would keep it in
> confidence. I know that I didn't tell you directly that
> I needed you to, but you are my closest friend, and I
> would hope that anything I share with you would be kept
> between us.

You can see that this statement only goes over what happened, and what our expectations were. It doesn't get into everything we feel and how angry we genuinely are, and that's what makes it more approachable. If we keep our emotions out of the discussion at first, the other person will be able to hear our side and offer their view of the situation. However, if we approach them with anger and hostility, we will only get the same in return. We won't know if there was a misunderstanding, or even if they are sorry and want to apologize. We can't resolve a conflict when we focus on why we are upset; repair and communication can only result if we stay calm and stick to the facts.

This technique can also be used when asking for something we need or want. I regularly tell my patients and viewers that for people to hear and understand us, we have to keep it simple. This can be applied to things like asking for a raise or even requesting that our spouse do their share of the housework. It can also help to write out our request beforehand and practice saying it. For example, let's say we believe we deserve a raise but struggle to find the words to ask for it. Let's start by writing out why we deserve it.

1. I have been with the company for over a year without a pay increase.

2. Since Frank left, I have been doing his job in addition to my own while we look for a replacement.

3. I have been told my work is exemplary in my past two performance reviews.

Always try to keep it to five bullet points or less. That way we can stick to the most important facts and not have the other person lose interest or focus. Then we put together what we want to say.

Hi, Gayle. I wanted to meet with you today because I would like to be considered for a raise. I have been with the company for over a year, I have been taking care of Frank's duties while we find his replacement, and I was told my work is exemplary on my past two reviews. Would you consider offering me a raise?

Keeping our emotions out of the equation when asking for something allows our concerns or requests to be heard and taken seriously. I know practicing may seem like a waste of time, but consider how many times you may have gone into a situation only to forget what you wanted to say. Or perhaps you completely chickened out and didn't even ask for what you needed. Whatever the case, it only helps us to write things out, practice saying them, and then go and do it. This ensures that we communicate what we mean clearly and set ourselves up to hopefully get what we want.

Be Empathic

When negotiating things in life, it helps if we can put ourselves in the other person's shoes. Only then can we understand why they feel the way they do, and how we can hopefully work together. This is something I try to do whenever I am frustrated with someone or a situation. For example, I had a small fight with one of my friends because I didn't invite her to my holiday party. Now, before you start thinking that I am a complete jerk, I knew she was going to be out of town visiting family, so I didn't even consider adding her to the list. Why send her an email about a party I knew she couldn't come to?

When we had lunch a few weeks later she told me that I hurt her feelings. At first I was shocked and found myself saying just how childish she was being. We got into a fight, and she left. I walked back to my car thinking the whole issue was stupid, and if she wasn't going to be able to come to the party, why did it matter if I invited her?

The next week she reached out and asked if we could grab a coffee. It was then that she explained that even though she couldn't go, it would have been nice to know she'd been invited. She also told me that when she was growing up, she never felt like she had a close friend, and would often get left out when someone was having a birthday party. She admitted that it was a bit silly and something she was working on, but because of her past, not getting invited was hurtful. After hearing why she felt so pained, I understood and apologized for getting upset.

If I had listened to her and allowed her to share her side, I could have avoided the fight altogether. By being open to hearing her side of the story, I could understand and we could talk it through. Now, don't think that just because I recognized her view and agreed to always include her that meant she was right and I was wrong. That's not the point of healthy communication. The goal is to be able to speak and listen to one another in a way that makes growth and connection possible. So if someone is open to seeing and hearing your side, you have to be open to reciprocating their effort.

If you find this tip challenging, here are some questions you can ask yourself to help you see a situation from another's perspective:

1. Was there something I said or did that could have been misinterpreted?

2. Was I clear when explaining what they could expect?

3. Did I follow through with everything I said I would?

4. Am I giving them time to explain why they are upset? Have I asked them?

Know that it's okay to struggle with this one. It's hard to open ourselves up to the idea that a misunderstanding could have been partially our fault. No one likes to be blamed for something going wrong; that's why we all have to work on communicating more and with more clarity. Putting yourself in someone else's shoes and giving them the time they need to explain their side can keep frivolous arguments at bay.

Taking Turns

I have this fantastic tool that I use in my practice whenever I am seeing families or couples. It can stop any fight right in its tracks, and even help spotlight unhealthy communication styles we may struggle with. It's by far my most useful tool, and all it is is a yellow laminated piece of paper called "the floor." I found this tool while reading the book *Fighting for Your Marriage*; it has been used by many therapists as a way to get people to take turns talking, so each person can be heard.[1]

The floor comes with a pretty simple set of rules we all should know and abide by but often don't. If you have the floor then you get to speak for yourself (no mind reading); you keep your statements brief and give the listener time to paraphrase what you just said. If you don't have the floor, then you must listen to what the speaker is saying and summarize what you hear (no arguing your side). In theory, it sounds pretty simple and easy to follow, but you would be surprised how many people struggle to follow the rules.

The hardest part for families and couples is to listen and only summarize what the speaker said. Everyone seems to want to fight back or tell their side of the story immediately! To have to wait until the floor is yours to share how you felt can feel like torture, and serves to show us how little we listen to one another. When we don't have to worry about fighting back right away, and we have to repeat back what we've heard, it can slow down, if not stop, an argument.

That's why this is another useful tool to practice on your own during any disagreement. Be quiet and let the other person speak, then tell your partner what you heard; after that you can feel free to share your personal thoughts on it. Just like this:

Speaker: "I was upset because I was trying to tell you how much easier it would have been to know you wanted to stay longer before I bought the flights to Florida. Then you said that I was having a meltdown, and that just made me feel worse."

Listener: "I hear you saying that I was late telling you how long I wanted to stay, and labeling your frustration as a meltdown was even more upsetting."

Speaker: "Yes. Exactly."

Now the floor is swapped between the partners.

Speaker: "Well, I didn't think what I was asking was that big of a deal, and hearing you be frustrated right away felt like an overreaction on your part."

Listener: "I hear you saying that my getting upset so quickly was surprising and more than expected."

Speaker: "Yes!"

While this practice can seem slow at first, it's not something we will have to do in such detail forever. It's just good practice to listen when someone else is speaking, ensure that you heard them, and then share your own side. When you interrupt or fight back right away, neither person gets to be heard, and both become even more upset. That's how some issues that seem like molehills can quickly turn into

> It's just good practice to listen when someone else is speaking, ensure that you heard them, and then share your own side. When you interrupt or fight back right away, neither person gets to be heard, and both become even more upset.

mountains, and can inevitably ruin our relationships. Using this technique can help us hear each other and feel listened to in return. You can use it with anyone in your life who is willing to try along with you. And don't think this only applies to marriages; I use this with my mom and friends all the time.

Be an Equal

This one seems to be getting harder every day with social media allowing for constant comparison. That doesn't mean we weren't comparing ourselves to others before the rise of social media, but now we don't even have to leave our house to do it. Whether we want to admit it or not, we can fall into the pattern of comparing ourselves to others in our lives. "Am I making more money than they are?" "Am I happier than she is?" "She's already married. I feel like such a loser." Whatever our hang-up, we look to those we are closest to for similarity, and if we don't see it, we judge.

We can judge ourselves and others based on who we think is doing best in a specific portion of life. The thing to remember whenever you find yourself spiraling down this judgmental black hole is that you can't ever have all the information. This means that all the numbers and factors we are taking into consideration are not based on fact; they are our own created fiction.

I call it fiction because we can't ever really know how someone is feeling and doing in life. We only know what they tell us and what we decide to believe. For that reason, it's vitally important that when communicating to those around us, we do it from a place of equality. Meaning no one is ever above or below anyone else. Now, I could get into my own philosophical beliefs about why this is always the case, but I am bringing it up in relation to communication. No one likes to be talked down to, and doing so will most definitely create conflict instead of growth.

Most commonly we think about this in reference to our work life. It can be hard to talk to someone we manage without seeming like an egotistical jerk. Don't fret; there are many ways we can recognize this issue and work to improve it. First, it can help to focus on the things you have in common with the person, which can help you connect and also communicate as their equal. It can also lead us into using some of the other tools we've talked about, like being empathic and hearing their side. Remember, we are all human and just want to be heard and spoken to with respect. Being paid more or having more power in a corporation doesn't make you more or less worthy of those things.

While this comes up a lot in our relationships with colleagues, it can also appear when we believe we are in the right in a situation. When we fail to use any of the other tools mentioned, especially putting ourselves in another's shoes, we may think that we are without a doubt correct. Communication is not successful when one party believes they are right and the other person is wrong. In fact, that's not communication at all: it's an argument. Connection is only successful when we put aside our assumptions and consider another person's perspective. To avoid this common misstep, consider these questions first:

1. Have I given them the opportunity to speak before making assumptions?

2. Did I attentively listen while they spoke?

3. Am I able to see my role in this and apologize where necessary?

4. Am I willing to give up on this relationship to be right?

Take some time with the questions and do your best to be honest. The fourth question can be tough to hear and take into consideration, but it's something we always need to ask when struggling to use this communication tool. If this tends to be your biggest stumbling block, try to remember that no one person can ever be a hundred percent right. There are always other perspectives and beliefs we cannot see or understand unless we listen. Without being open to hearing these differing points of view, we will limit the growth of our relationships and slowly become isolated.

Make It Personal

This communication tool is one you have most likely heard of if you have ever been in therapy. It's all about you, how you feel, and ensuring that you only speak for yourself. You guessed it: the dreaded "I" statements. While I know this tool is in many ways overused, it's still very effective. When we only speak for ourselves and don't blame others for how we feel, it leaves room for effective communication.

If you are not familiar with "I" statements, it's a way to take ownership of what happened and how we feel instead of blaming someone else. In short, rather than saying, "You make me feel so angry," you would say, "I feel angry because the dishes are not done!" It seems like a small change, but it can drastically affect the direction of a conversation.

The main point I want you to know about "I" statements is that they need to be focused on you and your experience. Using them properly means they assist you in sharing your feelings or view of things without opinion or judgment. Below are examples of how to properly and improperly utilize them.

Proper use:

- "I feel really sad about all of this."

- "I am not happy with what happened, and I am angry."

- "I would like it if we could talk this through without yelling."

Improper use:

- "I feel really angry at you because you are acting like a child."

- "I wish you would be more respectful to my parents."

- "Whenever you raise your voice I feel like screaming right back."

The common misunderstanding is that by using "I" to start or explain a situation, you are free to say whatever you want. You can see how that doesn't hold true, and even when we start out saying how we feel it can quickly turn into blaming and judging the other person. So it's best to take your time and ensure you are only speaking for yourself and about yourself.

The reason "I" statements are used so often in therapy is that when we blame others, there's a good chance they will get defensive. Once someone feels the need to defend themselves, they are shut down from hearing anything we say. Instead, they can start looking for holes in our argument or searching for past hurts that can help them build their case against us. For communication to be helpful, both people need to be able to hear what the other person is saying and feel heard themselves.

If we try our best not to blame the other person and instead communicate how we felt and what we thought took place, then we can work to understand each other. To show you how helpful this tool is, read the following statements and notice how you respond to each.

You always do that! I hate it when you act like that because you make me feel so stupid. I don't want to feel that way! Why do you have to make me feel like that?

versus

Whenever I hear things like "'You should've known" or "Why did you do it that way?" I feel hurt. I find myself second-guessing what I do, and often I feel stupid.

They elicit very different feelings. right? That's because the first one is filled with blaming statements, while the other is taking responsibility for how you feel while letting the other person know what upset you. Every time we communicate with someone about an upset we can choose one of these styles, and I assure you that selecting the second option will help your relationships develop and improve.

It's always hard to be told we need to change the way we interact in relationships, mainly because another person is involved and we have no control over how they decide to engage with us. That's why I encourage my patients to either do this work while in counseling together or to let the other person know what you are working on, and ask them if they want to try it with you. It can also be difficult because much of what we do can feel ingrained in us and almost like a knee-jerk reaction. That's why I always start off by asking my patients to notice how often they find themselves saying things like the following:

1. "You make me . . ."

2. "I feel that you . . ."

3. "I like that you . . ."

It's not that all of these statements are harmful every time they are used, but they can lead us into a more judgmental or blaming conversation. So just start noticing how often these words cross your lips during a disagreement or discussion with someone. Once we realize how often we do it and what it leads to, we can work to change how we communicate, one sentence at a time.

Ask Questions

Much of what causes us to be upset or even embarrassed comes from misunderstandings. I am certainly guilty of jumping to conclusions and being angry over what I decided must have happened. Taking the time to ask questions and genuinely listening to the answers can clear up most communication blunders.

I believe we struggle with this tool most because of the invention of texting. When you text someone, it can be read in a completely different way than you intended. Just think of the change in intonation between "So you like her?" and "So you *like* her?" In the second phrase the emphasis and a rise in our voice on the word *like* tells us the speaker is either teasing or thinks we like "her" romantically. When we miss out on bits of information like that, the sentiment of the entire conversation can be lost.

I know I've been guilty of jumping to conclusions, especially when I was dating in my early twenties. If it took a guy a day to text me back, I had already written him off and decided he wasn't worth my time. Never mind if he had a big project coming up or family was in town. There could be any number of things going on, but based on one interaction (or lack thereof) I had already decided what he felt, based on nothing but my racing mind and irrational beliefs. Trust me, none of these situations or relationships ended well.

So learn from my mistakes and take a minute to ask questions before jumping to conclusions. I know this tip may sound obvious, but just yesterday in my office a patient told me her mom hated her. She stated it with such conviction that it caught me off guard. I asked her if her mother had told her this recently, or what event prompted these feelings. All she said to me was "I don't know, I can just feel it. I felt it in the way she told me good morning and then left the house." I was shocked. Since when does telling a child good morning and then leaving for work constitute hating them?

Part of my therapist duties requires that I pose questions, and push through any defense mechanism or misinterpretation that may be in our way. In this case, it was my patient's faulty belief that her mother hated her. So I challenged her: "Have you ever asked your mom if she is upset with you or if she hates you?" My patient immediately became distressed. "Of course not! Why would I do that? I don't want to know how she truly feels!" *Ah-ha! Caught you!* That part I say in my head (for obvious reasons), but I get excited during these moments because I catch the real worry right away, and know just what we can do to fix it.

Long story short, her real worry was that her mom hated her, and since her mom had come into previous sessions as needed, we invited her to join us again. During that session, my patient was able to ask all the questions she worried about and get real answers. I had her repeat back what she heard her mom say and ensured she was taking it all in, and they both left the session feeling much better. In following up with my patient about this, we decided that it was best to ask those around us for information and validation before we chose to be hurt or angry.

I know it can be scary to ask questions sometimes. We often fear we are going to get actual evidence to support our misguided beliefs, but that's usually not the case at all. Much of what I see in my practice, and in my own life, is that by giving someone a chance to tell their side and explain what was happening, we often find it wasn't even close to what we expected.

Be Open to Compromise

As long as we strive to communicate and have healthy relationships, we will need to compromise. It can be small things like watching a movie you aren't that interested in or more significant things like moving so the other person can be closer to work. Whatever the case, finding a way to healthfully compromise is vital. Just like everything else we've discussed, it won't change overnight, and it will take practice. It can be hard to give up certain things we want and not be resentful. That's why it's so vital that we follow the steps outlined below when learning how to compromise with those in our lives.

First, assess what's being asked of you and how important it is. Is it something you feel you can give up today to get what you want tomorrow? Does it go against everything you believe? How does your giving in (or not) affect those around you? If even asking these questions seems silly, then it's probably not that big a deal and okay for you to give in to. If you need more time to think about it, then give yourself that time. It can also help to make a list of the things you aren't willing to give up. For me this list would be my career, adopting a dog, and trips to see family. Consider what's not up for negotiation in your life and write it down.

Second, know that it's not okay for you to always be the one who compromises. That doesn't solve the problem; instead, it creates a new one. When one person in a relationship always gives in to the other without receiving anything in return, it can lead to resentment. It can also unbalance the power in the relationship. Each member of any partnership should feel they have some power in it. I don't mean that we need to know we can control everything or have a lot of influence over the other person, but we must feel we have a purpose and belong in the partnership. Make sure that you are okay with giving something up, and that you aren't always the one to do it.

Third, know that every time you give up something, you have the right to negotiate for something else you want. If you are the one who gave in and decided to do what was best for you as a couple, you should then ask for something you want. Let's say that you want to spend New Year's Eve in the mountains. You have been planning it for months, saving money, and making arrangements. As the time gets closer, your partner tells you an old friend of hers is coming to town and she wants to stay home instead. You can decide to give in and say it's okay, but also ask that the following month you take a long weekend in the mountains. That way instead of one person feeling like they lost something, they can gain something at the same time.

Fourth and finally, never try to compromise while you're angry. In all truth, we can't do anything that well when we are mad. Anger doesn't allow us to see other perspectives or take sound advice. If we feel forced to make decisions about important issues while enraged, it will lead to more fights and resentment. We can wake up the next morning in a fog from the previous night's fight only to realize what took place and become upset all over again. Or we can pretend everything is okay for a while, only to bring it up years later. Waiting until we both feel calm and open to the other person will ensure that any compromise was made with a clear head and good intent.

It would be nice to live in a world where we all wanted the same things at the same time, but save yourself the stress and recognize it never happens like that. Instead, people have different plans, expectations, and desires. Many people will say compromise means everyone loses, but I choose to see it in a more positive light. Sure, we may not get exactly what we want at a specific time, but if we wait or do it differently, we get to experience it with those we love most. If we choose to work against those around us and demand things be done our way, then we can do everything we crave at the time that's best for us. But we would be doing it alone and in my opinion, that's too steep a price to pay.

Being Patient

We all crave connection with and understanding from those around us; it's human nature to seek out friendships and romantic relationships. I hope this chapter has shown you how you can keep those relationships happy and healthy. Communication is something we are all going to struggle with from time to time, but going back to these tips and tools should help you get back on track quickly.

As always, remember to be patient and kind as you try out these new techniques. We all have our own issues from our upbringing as well as old habits to overcome, so know that it's never perfect. What I am always reminding myself and my patients of is that we aren't striving for perfection; we are just hoping for improvement. If you are able to use one "I" statement instead of blaming someone for how you feel, you have accomplished a lot. Be proud, and keep pushing yourself to do it again.

chapter 10

Avoiding Common Mistakes and Healing Broken Relationships at Home, at Work, and in Life

No one is perfect. We are all going to get into fights, say and do things we don't mean, and upset those around us. Trust me, I am guilty of hurting those closest to me by not communicating well or lashing out when I am upset. This doesn't mean we can never have healthy relationships; all this tells us is that we need to notice what our biggest stumbling blocks are and work on them.

In the last chapter, I talked about how our inability to communicate appropriately as an adult often comes from issues in our childhood. This could be our parents not giving us proper attention, or someone abusing us. Whatever the cause, by working with the right mental health professional we can heal those past wounds so we don't feel the urge to act out of them anymore.

I talk about "processing through" and "overcoming" past wounds a lot, and the truth is that when we find ourselves acting out of situations from our past, the only way to stop doing it is to talk it through. This "processing" means that we need to find a professional we like and talk through what happened in detail until it's no longer emotionally upsetting. If we were severely traumatized, this might take a trauma specialist and a lot of work on our part, but by taking the time to acknowledge what happened and come to terms with it, we are then able to put it in our past.

We have to talk each upsetting situation through in detail because this gives our brain another chance to make sense of it and file it away. When something is traumatizing or extremely upsetting, our mind can get overwhelmed and not have time to neatly file away what just took place; parts of the memory are left lying around your file room floor waiting to be picked up and put away. That is what proper therapy does, and why it's best to work through issues with a professional. If we don't take the time to do this, the issues will keep cropping up whenever we are in a stressful or difficult situation.

Once we have overcome and filed away any past hurts, we can move on to noticing our unhealthy communication or relationship habits. It never helps to jump into changing things before knowing what we need to change. In a way, that would be like trying to hunt for something when you didn't even know what it looked like. Therefore, we first need to see which of the five most common communication mistakes we struggle with most, and then put together a plan to avoid making them in the future.

Keeping Score

When we keep score in a game, it's a way of telling who wins and who loses, but in a relationship it's the person who keeps score that always loses. If you haven't heard of the term *keeping score* before, it means that everything done or not done in a partner-ship is kept track of to see who's doing the most. For example, if I got up with the baby eight times this past week and you only got up three, I could use that against you in a fight. I am sure that just from this short definition you can see why keeping score is terrible for our relationships.

When we keep score, we change our connection with some-one else into a me-centered approach. Meaning that we only do things for them or our family as a way to elevate ourselves. Doing more isn't something we do with love or joy anymore; instead, it's a way to make us feel superior so we can prove that our partner isn't doing enough.

Keeping score can mean that whenever we do something that helps our partner or us out, there are strings attached. As if we only perform a kind act as a way to lord it over them or to get them to do things we want done. This behavior can lead to re-sentment, passive aggression, and unnecessary arguments. The good news is that there are some simple tips and tricks to help keep us from falling into this common trap.

First, if you decide to do something for someone else, do it because you want to. If you are worried that maybe you are doing it to prove you do more in the relationship, consider whether you enjoy being able to do this for them. Does the simple act of giving to them make you feel better and brighten your day? If you aren't sure or your answer is no, then it's most likely you're only giving to make yourself better by comparison. If you answer yes, and you get joy out of giving, then keep doing it.

When we give because we want to, it builds our connection to our partner and makes our relationship stronger. We can want to do something for them just because it will make things easier for them and in turn improve our life, but it still has to be done with love. The reason behind the gift is what creates the joy of giving.

It takes away any belief they aren't good enough or doing enough for the partnership, and instead shows you are in it together. Therefore, only give things to someone else when it comes from a joyful place, because that's when it will reinforce your bond.

Second, take a quick look at the things they have done recently. By considering what they have completed for you, you will kill any score you may have been keeping. In the same way that we talk back to any negative thoughts about ourselves, we can also talk back to any urges to keep score. If you find your mind wandering, looking for ways you have given more, also look for examples that prove they have done their share too. For instance, if I start thinking, "Why am I always the one who has to clean the bathroom. He never does anything to help out!" I then have to force myself to think of something like this: "He always cleans the floors and takes out the trash. It's so nice that I never have to do that."

Just like the exercise above can stop negative self-talk in its tracks, it can also prevent us from keeping track of everything that happens in a relationship. Know that we will all keep a record at some point, but that doesn't mean we are terrible people or that any partnership we get into is doomed to fail. It just proves we are human, and we have to work at our connection with others to ensure it's kept happy and healthy.

Building from the last technique, it can help to practice appreciation consciously. If we are looking for things we can thank our partner for, there won't be any room in our brain for keeping score. It also can change what we are looking for altogether, meaning that if we are always on the hunt for something they did that we are thankful for, our focus will be entirely on the positive. This small shift in our attention will not only improve our connection to our partner but also our overall mood.

Communication Filters

We all act from our life filters. Due to our past experiences, we may assume that situations will turn out a certain way without having any current evidence to support our assumptions. This can create conflict and upset where none should have existed. Here's a story from one of my viewers to help put communication filters into perspective:

> I am having a tough time dealing with my boyfriend, Joe. He's usually so nice and loving, but I think his drinking is getting out of hand! He was drunk last weekend on Friday, Saturday, and Sunday nights! So, on Sunday I dropped him off at his place, yelled at him and told him not to call me again. I know I overreacted, but drinking three nights in a row is a lot! He never does that, and I just can't take it. I know that I am extra sensitive because my dad was so abusive when he was drunk, and he was always drunk when I was growing up, but what if I end up just like my mom? I do not want her life! Now he's calling me all the time trying to figure out what happened, and I don't know what to do!

As you can see, because of her negative experience with alcoholism, this viewer is unable to accept one weekend of binge drinking as okay, and her reaction is out of proportion to the situation. That's why she feels lost and is trying to figure out what to do. When we are filtering everything in our lives through our past experiences, life can feel safe and predictable, but doing so also limits our ability to create new and varied memories. By continuing to give in to our existing filters, we are agreeing with the beliefs that come along with them, never giving ourselves the opportunity to see a different outcome. We inadvertently keep proving that it's always going to turn out the same way and why people, us included, can't change. That's a dangerous place to be while in a relationship; people can always try harder and change. That's what this entire book (and my career) is about!

I find the fact that we can change, grow, and break free from our past exhilarating! This means that all the things that happened to us don't have to control us forever. We just have to recognize what filters we have and where they come from. It may take you some time to figure all of that out, but here are some questions that have helped me:

1. What topics seem always to set you off or push your buttons?

2. Are there certain behaviors or situations you struggle to understand and get angry about easily?

3. How did your family communicate with each other about difficult topics?

4. How do you prefer to resolve conflict in your life?

5. While in a relationship, what expectations do you have of your partner? Do you express these to them?

Answering these questions may take some time and thought, but I hope it will get you thinking about how you were raised and how that may affect you today. It could even be something as simple as getting a gift for someone when you make an apology, or that shouting in your home growing up was not seen as fighting but rather a way of showing your passion for the topic. There are so many behaviors we see as normal or abnormal because of what we experienced growing up. Taking note of these and under-standing which of them affect our relationships in negative ways can help keep us from making the same mistakes our parents did.

Everyone seems to be afraid they will turn out just like their mother or father, but the truth is we only do that when we don't take the time to recognize their mistakes. I don't mean we need to call up our parents and ask them why they did things the way they did, or force them into explaining their mistakes. Instead, consider where your parents came from, what they struggle with today, and why they may have decided to do things the way they did. Our parents are human too, and probably didn't always know what they were doing. Not to mention they also come from a different generation with its own set of hang-ups and issues. Taking all of this into consideration can sometimes help us better see their problems.

Since we've addressed how our past can affect us, let's take a look at more current situations. Have you had an awful relation-ship where you were lied to or cheated on? Or perhaps you've had some friendships end because of how directly you commu-nicated to your friend. We have our own life experiences outside of the home we grew up in, so take some time to consider what filters you may have acquired on your own. Those also play a role in how we interact with those around us.

Once you have successfully identified a few of your most com-mon filters, I want you to notice when you are acting from them, and whether they are helping or hindering your relationships. If you find they are preventing your connections from flourishing, it's time to eradicate them. These filters usually cloak themselves in assumptions we make, and to get rid of them we have to ask questions for clarity, and seek to understand the situation entirely.

If asking questions doesn't quite work with your current situ-ation, you can also try to see it from the other's perspective. Let's practice this with our first example. If my viewer had already known that drinking was an issue and filter for her, she could have tried to see things from her boyfriend's point of view before yelling at him. Maybe he'd just watched his favorite football team win a big game, or was enjoying time with a friend who came into town for a birthday. He may not usually drink multiple days in a row because he doesn't feel the need to, but enjoys celebrating significant events with those he cares about. Taking the time to understand what the other person was thinking can help us recognize our skewed perceptions and keep them in check.

Never Say Never

Extremes and absolutes are easy to get into the habit of using, especially when we are upset. The types of statements I am referring to are those used to place blame on and judge someone else. Phrases like "You never take me on dates anymore!" or "Why do you always have to make me feel bad?" We have all heard or voiced these types of comments to those we were in relationships with, and I think I speak for us all when I say they didn't resolve or improve anything.

Speaking in absolutes is not helpful because it separates us from the other person and negates anything positive they have contributed to the relationship. By using extreme language, we are stepping away from the partnership and trying to blame them for our problems or upsets. The good news about this common misstep is that it's easy to spot, and therefore simple to fix.

As expected, begin by paying attention to any absolute language when speaking to those you care about. The most common words to be aware of are *always, never, can't, hate, wouldn't,* and *couldn't.* If you find one flying carelessly out of your mouth, stop, take a breath, and start the sentence over. Some easy replacement options are *possibly, sometimes,* and *maybe,* so feel free to use those instead.

It can even help to utilize those incredible "I" statements again and start conversations with "I feel . . ." or "We could try . . ." instead of accusatory language. Like we talked about before, by using a more personal style of communication, we can create conversation and understanding instead of argument. It also helps to notice when we make these types of statements to ourselves, and change them as well. Doing so can improve the friendship we have with ourselves, which I believe is the most important relationship we have.

Fighting Doesn't Mean a Breakup

Whenever we argue with someone in our lives, we have a choice to make. We can either be patient, hear their side, and do our best to come to an agreement or compromise, or we can stand our ground, talk down to them, and try to bend them to our will. While there are always going to be other things going on in our lives that affect our ability to think clearly, we should try our best to enter into a disagreement knowing it will be okay. This doesn't mean that we have to allow anyone to mistreat us or force us to do what they want. But we should be able to see both sides and work toward something that helps both of us, knowing that in the end we love and care for one another and will do our best to work through it.

Threatening statements like "I will divorce you so fast . . ." or "Maybe we should just break up then . . ." not only erode the trust and safety we should have in a relationship, but they also stop any compromise or resolution from happening. So long as there are no issues of infidelity, lying, abuse, or extreme incompatibility, I don't believe a period of distress should lead to a breakup. Every relationship is going to have its ups and downs, and if we find ourselves always running from them whenever it gets tough, we will see ourselves going from one failed relationship to another.

To stop ourselves from continuing to run away from conflict, we have to admit that we are scared. Scared of being vulnerable, or open enough to a real connection and conversation that might result in our feeling hurt. I used to be so afraid of getting hurt that I never let anyone genuinely get to know me. I still remember sitting in therapy lamenting the end of another relationship and giving my therapist all the reasons why it was over. My therapist listened and nodded along, and when there was a break she said, "You know what, Kati, you are a puffer fish." "A what?" I asked. "You are a puffer fish, which is soft and sensitive, so whenever anyone gets too close, you stick out your spines to keep yourself safe, and to keep them away. You just puffer-fished your last boyfriend."

I laughed when she first brought this up because as an analogy it was humorous, but it stuck with me (pun intended). She was entirely right. I had been puffer-fishing people for years, and I didn't even realize it. It took me many more sessions, but I finally figured out what was causing this reaction. I had been in a very tumultuous relationship throughout high school and much of college. I was lied to, cheated on, and in the end I turned into a version of myself I am not proud of. I refused to date for years after that breakup, and swore I would never let myself get hurt like that again.

In my mind, the only way to keep that promise was not to let anyone get too close. If they didn't know me entirely, then they couldn't do any harm, and thus began my pattern of puffer-fishing. After this realization, my therapist sent me home with some homework: to journal about my protective urge and think about how it affected my relationships. This homework took me many weeks, but after thinking about it I realized that by keeping everyone at arm's length, I was setting myself up to always be alone and feel misunderstood. And I didn't like that one bit. So I went back to therapy to find out how to stop being overprotective of myself.

This process took me a while and many slips-ups, but I first had to figure out what characteristics people in my life needed to have for me to consider letting them in. These were traits like honesty, consistency, and patience. From that point on, if someone showed me they didn't have one of these by lying or flaking on our plans at the last minute, I knew they weren't the right person to let in. However, if they showed they embodied those traits, I would start sharing small bits about myself as I felt comfortable. Sure, I would feel the urge to push them away from time to time, but since I knew where this was coming from, I was able to drive past it and keep moving forward.

I know my puffer fish story may not apply directly to your struggle with wanting to break up after every fight, but remember that relationships are never going to be perfect, and we will fight with those we care about most because they are closest to us. What solidifies our connection to others is the ability to disagree and be upset, yet choose the relationship over the fight. Give yourself the opportunity to let people in, allow them to get to know you, and lovingly deal with any disagreements. Working through those tough situations will bring us closer to those we love—but we have to choose to let it.

Healing Past Hurts

Those are the four most common communication mistakes for a reason; many people make them in their lives each day. If you find yourself struggling to move past any missteps in your relationships, don't worry. Along with the communication tools and techniques we talked about in chapter 9, there are some other ways to help us move past the pain or overcome any mistakes we may have made.

The first is to apologize. I know this may be hard if you think the other person did more harm and needs to apologize first, but if you are serious about continuing the relationship, then you may have to go first. Only apologize for what you feel you did wrong, and make sure you don't use the occasion to bring up anything else that may be upsetting you. An apology is supposed to end a fight, not start another one.

Second, let them in a little bit. What I mean by that is tell your partner why you have been so hurt or upset. Express to them the real reasons behind it, and why you acted the way you did, maybe by saying something like this:

> Leslie, I just wanted to let you know why I acted the way
> I did, and why what happened was so upsetting to me.
> See, when you said you were going to come with me to
> that big work event and then canceled at the last minute, I
> wasn't just upset about that. I feel like your canceling last
> minute has been happening more and more recently. You
> know, my mom used to do that sort of thing to me all the
> time as a kid, and I found myself feeling like that angry
> kid again. I think that's why I acted childishly and lashed
> out at you. I know that isn't an excuse, but I just wanted
> you to know why I was so hurt.

I find this level of honesty can soften any hardened heart, so consider sharing a bit more to help your loved one better understand you. Letting them in can also help them see your side for a bit and hopefully give them an opportunity to apologize as well, although that's not the goal but often a nice side effect.

Third, acknowledge your own need for change. This tool may take some preparation, but consider what caused the relationship to derail, and what you could do to prevent it from happening again. Take a look back at this chapter and the one before it for ideas. Are there patterns you can see in your relationship experience? Were you never taught how to communicate properly? Figure out what areas of your life need improvement and start working to make them better. You could even let your partner know what you are focusing on.

Letting them know what you are working on and why you are giving them an opportunity to do it with you will tell you if they are invested in the relationship as well; if they're not, doing this upfront will save you a lot of time and effort. Like we talked about before, both members of a partnership need to be invested in its improvement for any lasting change to take place. If you are only going to be making improvements to yourself, it's best to know that in advance.

Last, decide to let it go. This could be moved to the top of this list, but I find that many of us need to go through the other steps first before we can make this commitment. When we hold on to past pain for too long, we can look back to find it's been keeping us prisoner. Therefore, to put a recent hurt behind us, we have to consciously release ourselves from it and promise not to go back.

This means that we will no longer allow our thoughts to carry us back to that fight and replay it over and over until we are so upset we can't even look at the other person. We must also agree to not bring up any past upsets during current disagreements. I know this is easier said than done, and it's expected that we will slip up and try again, but that's why it's the final step in healing. To entirely move on from the past, we have to leave it where it happened, and not reinjure anyone, or ourselves, with something we cannot change.

Communicating Needs at Work

Since our communication needs don't end with friendships or romantic relationships, it's important that we also address work needs. If we find ourselves needing to take time off or express an upset to a co-worker, there are some important things to factor in before starting the conversation in the workplace.

Let's start by addressing the need for time off. If we are having a hard time with our personal life and need to take some time to care for it, we will need to talk to our human resources (HR) department. The one thing to consider when talking to HR is that they are in place to protect the company you work for; they are there to handle all the hiring, firing, training, and benefits. Remembering they are there to protect the company as a whole is important because we shouldn't tell them more than we need to. They may be friendly and helpful people, but what we need to worry about and protect is our job and their belief in our ability to do it.

Since we have to keep in mind that we need our job and want HR to think we can still do it, we should only tell them the bare minimum. I always have my patients tell their employer that they need to take a medical leave because of health concerns. That's where we start, and that will ensure you get the proper paperwork for your time off. Then you can take it to your therapist, psychiatrist, or doctor to fill out. Your HR department doesn't have the right to ask you a lot of questions about what's going on, what you are struggling with, or much of anything. That's what the paperwork is for, and why I encourage my patients to tell them they will have their medical professional fill it out so HR gets all the information they need. Leave it at that.

I don't say all this to scare you or make you think you will be fired because of a mental illness, but there is still a stigma surrounding it as a whole. I have had too many patients and viewers tell me they have been fired or demoted because of their struggles, and although it's technically illegal, that doesn't mean your employer won't find ways around it. So to keep everyone safe and employed, only share that you may need to take a medical leave, and ask for the proper paperwork. Have a mental health or other health professional fill it out, then take it back in.

I also encourage you to talk with your boss briefly about your leave. Again, just tell them you are having some health issues and need to take some time off. Since they are your boss, they should know from you directly what's going on and that you will be out of the office for a bit. I would keep it simple and to the point:

Hey, boss, I just wanted to let you know that I have been having some health issues of late and just popped into HR to find out how I can take a medical leave to take care of them. I am not sure how long I will be out, but I will keep you updated as I figure out the dates. Hopefully, I can return to work quickly and feeling much better. Thank you for your understanding.

Keeping it short and to the point will prevent us from oversharing. As with other tools and techniques we have talked about, I also recommend you rehearse saying this out loud to yourself or someone else. That way you can practice how you want to say it; you can even role play what they might ask or answer back. Then when you go in to speak with your boss and the HR department, you will be confident and ask for what you need.

The last bit of advice I have about taking time off from work is to structure that time. I don't mean you need to be busy every day, but set small goals, structure your days with your therapist, or get into a more intensive therapy program. Taking time off can be great, giving us the breathing room we need to heal and feel better overall, but not having anything to do can also cause us to feel worse. Planning our treatment as well as time with friends and family can ensure we don't start to worsen or isolate ourselves.

Also, there are often wait lists for treatment facilities, so if that's something you are looking into, make sure you set it up before you take time off. Planning out our much needed leave before taking it can ensure we make the most of the time we have. Fitting self-care into each of your days can help improve your mood and give you simple daily to-dos. Do whatever you need to make the most of your time off, because having the ability to work on your mental health full time can change your life, and I want you to take advantage of it!

Dealing with Co-Workers

While many of the tips discussed earlier can be applied to co-worker relationships, there are a few extra things we need to consider. First, it doesn't matter if we don't like someone we work with. Our colleagues aren't necessarily people we want to be friends with, and whether or not we get along shouldn't affect our ability to work alongside them. We have to find the best way to work together even if they aren't someone we would pick to have as a friend.

The best way to remedy any issue at work is to stop the problem quickly before it turns into something bigger. This means communicating more than you would typically, and working through any disagreements as soon as they come up. Don't allow a problem to fester overnight or go unaddressed. This doesn't mean we should be aggressive toward anyone we work with, but that we be direct about what's going on. For example, if we have differing opinions on how a meeting should be structured we could say something like this:

> I can see you would prefer us to have the review portion
> earlier than I would, and we both want to teach the
> technology section. How about we compromise and you
> can have the review portion when you want, and I get to
> teach them how to use the new tools. Sound fair?

Quickly working to find a way to move past any disagreements will make it easier for us to continue working together. This will also prevent us from having discussions with our boss about it, and save them the headache of having to deal with a complicated work relationship. Overall, if we can figure out a way to work together, even if we disagree, it makes everyone's life easier.

If we are way past an easy compromise, and our issue with a co-worker has made our job more difficult, or possibly even prevented us from completing our work every day, we will have to take it to our boss or HR department. While this should be a last resort, if we find ourselves in this position, there are some tips to keep in mind that can make it easier for all involved.

To ensure you don't forget what you want to say, or say something you don't mean, it can help to write it all out first. Then simplify it into three to five bullet points describing what has happened and why you haven't been able to resolve the issue on your own. Practice saying these things out loud and imagine what your boss or HR person would reply. Doing this will not only prepare you for your meeting but also help you get out any anger or aggression you may feel. You want to come across as cool, calm, and ready to fix the problem.

Also, check that what you are going to say isn't judgmental or rude, stick to the facts, and work toward a solution with them. This will protect not only your job but also your reputation. Last, prepare what you would say if the person you are having difficulty with asks you about this. If you work in a small office, they may guess you were the one who talked to their boss or HR and confront you about it. So you are not caught off guard, plan to say something like "Hi Cheryl, yes, I did speak with HR because of our issues working together. I hope we can figure out a way to overcome this so we can continue doing our jobs." Depending on how this person is, you may want to get up and walk away at that point or ask them if they want to talk about it.

If you ever fear for your safety or are being bullied, it's best to only converse with this person when other employees or an HR representative are present. Hopefully, we are all able to work out our issues with our co-workers, but if the environment at our office isn't good for our mental or physical health, there is never a good enough reason to stay. Begin updating your résumé and looking for another place where you can enjoy what you do and the people who work alongside you.

No Human Resources!

I know that many of us work in companies that don't have an HR department, and we may be left to work a problem out on our own. If that's the case, there are still some things you can do to try and keep the arguing and upset to a minimum.

First, no trash talking. When we talk poorly about someone else, it not only makes us look bad but it can also make us feel bad. Focusing on the negative things about someone else shifts our attention from positive or happy situations and instead causes us to only notice things going wrong or mistakes being made. Over time this can cause us to struggle to see anything positive going on around us, and make us look like the employee responsible for all the trouble. Keep your comments to the point and avoid making judgments.

Second, feelings can be different from actions. Just because we don't get along doesn't mean we need to behave badly. There is a big difference between not liking someone and treating them poorly. Find other ways to express what you are feeling outside of work, like taking a fitness class or venting about work to your therapist. Do whatever you need to do to keep your feelings about your co-worker to yourself while you're at work. Acting on those feelings will only make things harder.

Third, kill any issue you may have with kindness. If they are being difficult and have decided to yell at you about how you set something up, be nice about it. Smile, offer to change things to their liking, or be open to doing things their way. By taking the high road you not only look more respectful and adult, but they in turn seem more childish and unprofessional. I know it can be difficult to be nice when someone is rude, but grin and bear it. Remember, this isn't your personal life; this is work, and unfortunately, we don't get to pick who we work with.

Last, know it's okay to not like someone. There are so many types of people in the world, all with their own set of preferences and issues; it is not possible to get along with everyone. The sooner we allow ourselves to accept that, the better we will all feel. However, if we must work with someone we don't like, it can help to limit the amount of time we spend with them, choose other projects they are not part of, and focus on our own work. By lessening the amount of time we have to be with them every week, we can save ourselves from feeling burned out or dreading work altogether.

You Can Only Do Your Best

Whether you have many healthy relationships in your life or are just trying to make one work, with practice it gets easier and better. Any partnership is going to take effort from both sides for it to function adequately, and I hope that with the tools and tips given, you will feel able to hold up your end.

Learning new techniques can be difficult, and you will slip up and fall back into old habits, but keep trying. As you improve and become more comfortable using these communication skills, you will find yourself in fewer disagreements and feel better over-all. Everyone deserves happy and healthy relationships, so give yourself the chance to cultivate them. By doing so you will see just how rewarding connections with others can be, and finally feel supported and loved by those around you.

Also, remember that you can let yourself in and out of any relationship that isn't working. I say this because we often stay in unhealthy relationships much longer than we need to, and while we can do our best to avoid communication blunders, if the other person isn't willing to work with us, we don't have to stay. Do your best to be fair, and try to let them know what's going on, but if things only seem to get worse, know that someone can only make your life unpleasant if you let them.

chapter 11

Help! I Am in Therapy and Still Struggling!

How to Get More Help When We Need It

Often seeing a therapist once a week just isn't enough. We may notice there is just too much to talk about in our weekly sessions, and we never feel we are caught up on all that's going on. We could even start to slip back into old, unhealthy habits, or find that our current struggles are getting worse. I know these experiences can feel terrible, but they are very common, and they let us know we need more professional help than we are receiving. The good news is that there are many options available; we just have to know what they are and how to ask for them.

There are five red flags I look for in my practice that are warning signs a patient needs more help. The first, as I mentioned, is finding that the time allotted to therapy isn't enough. If we can't work through what happened that week, let alone get into all of our past issues, we may need more support. I like to think of therapy during this time as treading water: we aren't able to get where we are going, but we aren't drowning in our symptoms either. Therapy should progress; we need to feel we are working toward our goals at a slow but steady pace.

It's also important to understand that we will all go through periods in therapy when we feel like we are just treading water. It's normal to struggle to keep up when things get stressful or overwhelming, and needing more help may only be temporary. I was taking a break from therapy when I got engaged, but the stress of working two jobs and planning a wedding sent me right back in. I even went in two times a week for a few months until I felt better able to manage everything going on. Everyone will go through periods when they need to add in another session, or change their treatment plan entirely, and the sooner we make those changes, the better.

A second red flag is the strong urge to go back to an unhealthy coping skill. This could be an urge to use an addictive substance, or even an impulse to start a fight with someone we love. Bad habits can be easy to fall back into, so notice if they are on your mind more often than not, and make sure you reach out for some extra support as needed. The sooner we get the help we need, the less likely we are to act out in an old and unhealthy way.

Third, it's also a red flag when we can't talk about what we need to because it's too difficult. This doesn't mean that having a hard time with a painful memory or situation indicates you immediately need a higher level of care. However, if you aren't able to talk about it at all, and it's not getting any easier, it may be best for you to look into a more supportive environment. Adding in groups or joining a more intensive treatment center can help us feel more safe and comforted, and allow us to talk about what we've been through.

This red flag is often the hardest and most frustrating for patients and therapists alike to deal with. That's because we like our therapist and are getting help for certain things we want to work on, but the real root of our struggles remains. We can try and try to work through it and process all that happened, but we just can't. That's why it's so vital that we reach out for more support, whether it be longer or more frequent sessions with our current therapist, a more intensive day program, or even inpatient. Finding the right treatment will help us genuinely benefit from therapy and get to the root of our issues.

The fourth red flag is struggling to tell our therapist the truth. I have had many patients lie in every session about how they are doing on their own. I believe them when they tell me they are doing all the homework, eating properly, and sleeping well, only to discover months later that it's all been a lie. I will often find out because a parent comes in for a session and lets me know what's been going on at home, or I notice the progress my patient should be making doesn't match up with what I see in my office.

When I confront my patients about my concerns, they usually say they just wanted me to be proud of them, or they were afraid I would refer them to a treatment center. Whatever the reason, if you aren't able to tell your therapist the truth about how you are doing, you may need to consider other care options. Also, it's important to note that this can apply in the opposite way as well, meaning that you pretend you are doing worse than you are in order to stay at a certain treatment level. Either way, it's a sign that you need a different degree of professional help, because where you are now isn't the right fit.

The fifth and final red flag is not being able to function in our daily life. Inability to function means we struggle to get to work or school, we are unable to socialize or connect with those we love, and we aren't able to properly take care of ourselves. This may sound extreme, and is obviously a sign that we need more help, but you would be surprised by how many people don't realize how bad things have gotten until someone else mentions it. Also, if we are isolating from those we care about, our inability to take care of things can go unnoticed until someone finally comes to our home or our therapist points it out.

When we find ourselves unable to keep up with the requirements of life, we will need to get more professional support quickly. Since this is a more extreme concern, help will most likely be inpatient or at least a day program. I know there are a lot of different types of treatment out there and their names or acronyms don't always make sense, so let's define what options you have and what the differences are.

Treatment Options

As a disclaimer, remember that I am a therapist who was trained and is practicing in the United States in the state of California. All my experiences and knowledge about the systems of care come from where I have worked and who I have worked with over the years.

Whenever we find ourselves having a hard time and decide to reach out for some professional help, it's nice to know we have various options available, depending on our need. I know we talked briefly about levels of care in chapter 3, but it's essential that you know what each title or acronym means when it comes to the amount of time—from outpatient half-days to full-time live-in—that would be spent at a facility, and what you can expect. While it may still be hard to decide what's best for us at the time, try to consider these few things first: what you can afford, your ability to keep up with various activities in your life, how often you wish you could attend therapy, and if you are able to take time off.

When it comes to taking time off, I want to focus on the word *able,* meaning that, yes, it sucks to take a year off from school or have to do the paperwork to take a medical leave from work, but you can do it. Too many times I've had patients and viewers who put off getting the level of care they needed because they were afraid to take time off. If you are fortunate enough to be able to do it, make it happen now, because life doesn't get better without our putting in the time and effort.

Outpatient

The word *outpatient* comes from the hospital setting, as most mental health terminology does, and *Merriam-Webster's Collegiate Dictionary* defines it as "a patient who is not hospitalized overnight but who visits a hospital, clinic or associated facility for diagnosis or treatment." This type of treatment can apply to pretty much any care you receive while still going about your daily life. This could be your weekly therapy session or monthly check-up with your psychiatrist. It's done on a regular basis, but you only go in for treatment for your allotted time and leave afterward.

Outpatient treatment is the type of care I offer in my private practice. My patients come in for their hour or two each week and are able to manage their life in between our sessions. Aside from the random emergency, they are able to take what we work on in therapy and apply it to their life. They can care for themselves and handle their responsibilities; they just need some weekly support and guidance.

Most people start with outpatient since it's the easiest to fit into their schedules and the lowest level of care. Also, it's only an hour or so a week; therefore, if you are nervous about telling people in your life about it, no one has to know you are going. If you find you are okay seeing someone briefly each week, and you are able to work on what brought you in, then I would say it's a good fit and you are getting the level of care you need. If not, don't worry; there are many more options available.

Intensive Outpatient Program (IOP)

If we have tried increasing our outpatient sessions and are still feeling like our struggles are getting the best of us, the next step up is an intensive outpatient program (IOP). Some people may call them intensive outpatient treatment (IOT), but because IOP is a much more widely used term and both phrases mean the same thing, we will call all treatments of this level IOPs.

IOPs usually focus on a specific issue, meaning that each program you hear about will offer treatment for a different mental illness. Some specialize in eating disorder recovery, others focus on addiction, and many help people suffering from depression. Whatever your issue, make sure you choose a program that is right for you. IOPs can offer anywhere from ten to twenty hours of treatment services in three to five days each week. During that time you may see a therapist one on one, engage in group therapy sessions, see a psychiatrist or general medical doctor, and possibly see a dietitian. In short, it's a one-stop shop for all your treatment needs. Each facility will have their own schedule and program, so it's important to ask what they offer and how many hours and days a week you need to devote to it.

Many of my patients have been able to keep their full-time jobs or continue attending school and still go to their IOP. Therefore, this is an excellent option for those of us who aren't able to take time off, but still need more support. Also, insurance companies tend to cover this level of care completely, or with a small deductible, making this choice even more accessible. If an IOP isn't helping, and you are still feeling like you are just barely keeping your head above water, there are still more treatment options to look into.

Partial Hospitalization Program (PHP)

The next step in options for professional mental health care is a partial hospitalization program (PHP). These are often offered at the same clinics where IOP treatments take place, and are mostly the same as an IOP but with more frequency and intensity. Instead of three to five days, these programs run for five to seven days a week, and you are expected to be at the clinic for most of each day. PHP is a great option if we are experiencing an increase in our symptoms and our condition continues to worsen even with some professional care. PHPs are the highest level of care we can receive while still living on our own.

Whenever I refer patients to a PHP, I let them know that for them to get the most out of their treatment, they need to treat it like their recovery is their job. Putting in all the time and effort we can at this stage can help keep us out of the hospital and able to still have some freedom. If we find ourselves needing this level of care it means that we are unable to function for a majority of our day, and are doing our best to stop a relapse or more severe presentation of symptoms. The overall goal of PHP is to help patients better manage the symptoms of their mental illness so they can feel better and get back to their life.

Another way a PHP can be utilized is as a step down from inpatient treatment or hospitalization. Meaning that if we had been treated at a higher level of care for months, we would then move into a PHP so we could return home and slowly integrate back into our life. The hardest part for many of my viewers and patients is having to go back to their regular life because of its many triggers and issues. Doing this slowly, stepping down one level of treatment at a time, allows them to have support as they navigate through this transition.

Inpatient/Residential Treatment

When spending most of our days in treatment still leaves us feeling bad and struggling to cope, living at a facility is the next step. Residential programs have very structured days and nights, where you are expected to be somewhere doing something at all times. I don't say this to make them sound scary, but needing this level of care means you receive constant support and help around the clock. They have a busy schedule in place to keep you feeling supported and safe every day.

I worked at an inpatient eating disorder treatment center for many years where patients' days were planned out by the hour; many patients couldn't be left alone at all. All the women at the clinic had to be up and eating breakfast at a certain time, and each meal could only last a specific number of minutes. We would then move from group therapy sessions to individual ones. Going into a treatment center at this level means you give up most of your freedom in order to get better. Of course, you can leave at any time, but if you stay you are expected to follow the rules and participate in the program.

These centers have strict rules to keep you safe from whatever you are struggling with. If we need this level of support, it's because we can't trust ourselves to make good decisions, and we need someone to be there all the time to ensure we make healthy and productive choices. During one of my first full days at the treatment center, I was responsible for the "obs" (short for observation) of one patient. I had to follow her around after every meal observing her every move. I know that may sound crazy, but this was to make sure she didn't purge or engage in any other eating disorder behavior; in other words, to help her recover more quickly. It was super uncomfortable for both of us, since this could even entail going with her to the restroom or sitting next to her while she called her mother.

By giving up our freedom to make choices we recognize that we can't do it on our own. This doesn't mean we are weak or sad, but instead shows that we realize how developed our illness has become and that we need around-the-clock professional care to get rid of it. We wouldn't judge anyone for going into the hospital for days or weeks to treat their pneumonia, and mental illnesses shouldn't be thought of any differently. Choosing to get a higher level of care is difficult, shows a magnitude of strength, and is something we should applaud.

Hospitalization

There are a few main reasons why we would need to consider hospitalizing ourselves or someone we love. The first is that they are a danger to themselves, which means they are actively suicidal and cannot be left alone for fear they will try to kill themselves.

This is usually something a mental health professional will recognize first and ensure the person gets to the hospital for treatment immediately. However, if you or someone you love has the means to harm themselves, a plan to do it, and is showing signs they may act soon, please take them to a hospital right away; it could save a life.

The second is that they are a danger to others, meaning they are seriously considering killing someone else. If they are in treatment, their therapist or other mental health professional will get the police or other forces to take them to a hospital and hold them there for a few days. They will also warn the possible victim and try to get them the help they need until the emergency passes.

I know both those reasons seem extreme, but as mental health professionals we are legally mandated to ensure that if someone is a danger to themselves or others, they are placed in a hospital and kept safe. I have heard from many viewers that being forced into treatment is terrible and not very therapeutic, but at that point it's just about safety. Therefore, even if you aren't quite ready to go to the hospital, you may be forced to.

The third reason we may need to be hospitalized is that our symptoms have caused us to need not only mental health care but also intensive physical care. For example, many of my patients with eating disorders will not reach out for outpatient treatment until they are very physically ill, which isn't something I can help with. For this reason, I always require that they get a full physical before I take them on as a patient, and if they need just as much medical care as they do mental health care, then a hospital is the best place for them.

The final reason we may want to consider going to a hospital for our mental health treatment is that we feel it's best that we are forced to continue. Some of my past patients struggled to stay at residential facilities, and when the recovery process became too much, they checked themselves out. When we sign up for hospital treatment, we are often on a locked floor within the building and unable to leave without a professional's consent. Naturally, every program is different, but many function that way, so it's crucial that we understand the rules and regulations before signing up for hospital treatment.

Last, know that not all areas of the world have both inpatient options as well as hospital-based programs. Many people find themselves with access to either outpatient or hospitalization options and have to choose accordingly. Just know that the level of care you need during different periods of your life is something only you can recognize. Be honest with yourself and those who are trying to help you, and start the appropriate treatment right away.

What Is Relapse?

The term *relapse* is something we tend to attribute only to addiction treatment. However, it can apply to many other issues. If we are working on our depressive symptoms and we feel them improving for a while, only to go through a stressful period and have them come back, that would be considered a relapse. Per *Merriam-Webster's Collegiate Dictionary*, the definition of relapse is "the act or an instance of backsliding, worsening, or subsiding" and "a recurrence of symptoms of a disease after a period of improvement." You can see how this term can apply to many illnesses and problems. Here's an example of how relapse can sneak its way in:

I was so glad that I had started therapy and decided to start on an antidepressant too. I never knew I could feel this good, and I honestly don't know why I put it off for so long. I'm not sure when it happened, but after starting to feel a bit more tired each day and not wanting to do many of the things I used to love doing, I suddenly realized I was depressed all over again. How did this happen? I thought I was doing well and finally feeling like myself, and now I am worried that I am back to square one. Ugh!

The truth about relapse, or "slip-ups" as I like to call them, is that they happen to everyone. No one is perfect, and we shouldn't treat our mental health any differently than we do other parts of our life. You wouldn't expect to start a new job and never make a mistake, would you? You also wouldn't assume that you'd never disagree with someone you're dating, right? The same goes for our self-improvement. We will have times when things are going well, and other times when we will have to make a more concerted effort to keep getting better.

That's why it's important to recognize how we define the term relapse. Does it mean things have completely deteriorated and we are back to square one, or does it mean we just slipped up and need to get back on track? It could help to take a minute and consider how you define relapse, and possibly create your own unique definition. This can help us stay motivated when we are going through a tough time or even improve our self-talk when we need it most. If it's hard to get started, here are some prompts:

1. If someone told you they slipped up, what would you think that meant?

2. What would be the difference between a mess-up and a relapse?

3. What would you consider the opposite of relapse?

4. Are there times you feel you've relapsed? What did that look like?

5. How did you know a relapse had occurred?

This exercise may seem a bit odd or silly, but it can help us to examine our beliefs and definitions sometimes. That way we aren't too easy or hard on ourselves during our process. It can even help to perform this task with your therapist or other mental health professional. That way you can decide together what constitutes your needing more help versus your just needing to increase your self-care in between sessions.

The language we use to describe an experience is vitally important to proper care. We need to be able to express our feelings and have those who are helping us know what we mean. What may feel like a relapse to one person may just be a hard day to another. Knowing what our limits are, when we need more help, and what that looks like can ensure we get the support we need right away.

What Can Trigger a Relapse?

I hate the word *trigger* because it's been overused to the point where it can mean anything. But for the sake of this topic, trigger is the best term I can come up with to describe what can start the relapse process. Since everyone struggles with different issues in their life, there is no way to list every possible trigger and ensure we all avoid them. Instead, I would like to focus on how we can figure out our causes of relapse based on what we already know.

First, let's take a moment to look back to when you first started experiencing your symptoms or using that unhealthy coping skill. For example, when did you take your first drink, or use drugs for the first time? If that's not your type of struggle, when did you feel depressed for the first time? Or when did you have your first panic attack? Think back to the very first time you felt that way, and consider what else was going on in your life. Were there any stressors? Significant changes happening to you? If you don't know where to start, here's an example from one of my viewers:

I know this is going to make me sound crazy, but I remember feeling anxious even as a child. I have this vivid memory of me as a baby listening to my parents scream at each other and digging my fingers into the carpet in our home. I couldn't have been more than a year old, and I remember shaking and digging my fingers deeper and deeper into our ugly brown shag carpet. I never told anyone about that before, 'cause I've always thought that meant I was just born anxious. I still worry that it means I can't get better, that I am just supposed to be this way, but remembering that moment has helped me see that it may have just been my response to all the fighting. I find I still hate it to this day, and being around a loud argument can easily cause a panic attack.

I know not everyone is going to be able to uncover a memory from that far back, but you can see how spending the time to remember when we first felt a certain way or used a particular substance can tell us a lot about our triggers. In this person's case, it could have been raised voices or any argument. It could have even been being ignored; since his parents were fighting they probably weren't paying any attention to him, and that could have been upsetting.

Second, make a list of all the possible things that could have caused you to experience your first symptom. These could be situations, people, emotions you felt at the time, or even relationships you had. There is no need to be judgmental about this list, or worry that it's too long; it's better to include as many things as you can think of, and weed out the ones that don't apply later on. Give yourself time with this process; it can take a while to remember everything going on in our life at that time and sort it all out. Journaling about this can also encourage us to jot things down as we recall them.

The final step is to test out your list to see which items trigger you. No, I don't mean that you need to create these situations and possibly send yourself into a relapse; what I mean is that you need to look back at your last panic attack, drug use, etc. and see which potential triggers were present. Do a little personal research to see which of your list items were around most of the times you were struggling. After completing that task you will know which situations, people, or emotions create the most distress for you, and then you can take that to your therapist and figure out how to better manage them. Taking the time to work through these steps will help you better understand your issues and also prevent relapse from occurring again and again.

How to Prevent Relapse

If I'm honest, when someone tells me they are constantly triggered or easily upset by those around them, I know immediately that they have no idea of how to take care of themselves. I know that may come across as mean, but we are never able to control what other people around us do, and if we are allowing other people to have complete authority over how we feel, we have to change. While we will all have certain trigger situations or people who know how to push our buttons, for the most part we should be able to manage any upsets that come our way.

Once we identify what upsets us most and sends us sliding back into unwanted territory, we need to determine what our early pre-relapse signs look like. It could be that we cancel plans with friends, notice changes in our sleep, or observe the return of some unhealthy thoughts; whatever it is, pay attention. Knowing these signs is just as important as being aware of the triggers themselves, because if we are good at recognizing these right away, we can prevent most relapses. I know it can be hard to know what to look for, so here are some of the most common signs I have found with my patients:

1. Sleeping too much or struggling to sleep at all

2. Wanting to isolate (not socialize, canceling plans, shutting our phone off, etc.)

3. Feeling exhausted all the time

4. Eating too much or not enough

5. Not wanting to go to therapy or any support groups anymore (or not going at all)

6. Struggling to keep our thoughts focused on recovery

7. Thoughts about life and treatment start to become more negative

8. Urges to act impulsively or having a lot of impulsive thoughts

Hopefully, answering these questions will help get you started on figuring out what your signs and symptoms are because, trust me, everyone is going to be different.

Next, we need to beef up our self-care. I talk a lot about how important it is that we take care of ourselves, and that's because taking care of ourselves can change our lives. Making time to relax, recharge, and even being loving and careful with ourselves can give us the strength we need to thrive. One of the ways I like to explain the importance of self-care is by using the poker chip analogy.

Imagine that each morning when you wake up, you have eight poker chips. This is all you get for the day, and each time you encounter something stressful or complicated, it's going to cost you some of your chips. Let's say traffic is awful and you honk at three people on your way to work; well, that just cost you three of your eight chips. Then your boss tells you that report you've been working on is due a week early; you lose another two chips. It may not even be lunchtime yet, and you only have three chips left!

When we've run out of chips, we may lose ourselves completely. We could start crying, pick a fight with someone, or relapse into an old pattern of behavior we have been trying to change. Making time for self-care as often as possible allows us to wake up with more chips, or even pick up some more throughout our day. We can also get so good at caring for ourselves that we have a stockpile of chips, and can draw from them during really tough periods so we don't relapse. Most things in life will happen whether we want them to or not, so start preparing yourself for it—do something nice for yourself right now!

Many of my viewers and patients alike have a hard time figuring out what self-care means, so here are some ideas to help you create your self-care plan.

1. Go to bed early, or sleep in late.

2. Go for a walk.

3. Give yourself a foot rub.

4. Treat yourself to a massage.

5. Take a nap.

6. Get together with a good friend.

7. Pet an animal.

8. Turn off your phone for an hour.

9. Listen to your favorite music and dance.

10. Journal.

I could make a list for you that's over a hundred items long, but I hope that gives you a better concept of what your list could look like. Write down your ideas and try them out. It's essential that you enjoy them and feel that they fill you back up energetically, emotionally, and creatively. If you don't end up liking one of them, take that item off the list and add another one to try. Once you have a pretty solid list of five to seven things, make time for them each week. I know we all have busy lives, but making time for our health isn't going to be something we regret doing. In the same way we try to eat healthy food and exercise, think of this as diet and exercise for your mental health.

Next, we need to create a safety plan, because it helps to have a plan in place when we start noticing some of our relapse signs. That way we don't have to try and figure out what to do after we are already feeling a bit off; this can be done with a therapist or by yourself. The plan should include which self-care tools we need to use and for how long, as well as who we can reach out to when we need some extra support. Since I find talking about safety plans more difficult than just showing you one, there's an example on the next page.

Last, we need to reach out for help. I know this is woven into all stages of this process, but it's vital that you realize you are always worthy of getting more help. This could be calling your therapist and adding an extra appointment that week, or even texting a supportive friend in the middle of the night. Having the support of others can ensure that when we don't feel strong enough to keep fighting, we are able to sustain our recovery.

I hope you find these tips and tools helpful and easy to implement in your life. My goal is to always hope for the best but plan for the worst, and I believe that if we plan enough, maybe the worst doesn't have to be so bad, or even happen at all.

Recovery Is Possible

Everything in life worth having will take work, and recovery is no exception, but know that whatever your struggle is, you can overcome it. Many people talk about mental illness like it's incurable, as if it's something that will always affect our lives. I don't agree. The belief that we can't overcome our problems or strive for a better future is a very dark and dreary way to look at life. It fails to take into consideration how much strength and persistence each of us has, and I for one prefer to focus on that instead.

Yes, working on ourselves is difficult and can sometimes feel like we're taking one step forward and two steps back, but the good news is we can be sure that where we are headed is better than where we've been. I am always reminding my patients and viewers that we already know what it's like to live in the grips of

SAFETY PLAN

What symptoms or signs am I experiencing right now?

_____

_____

_____

Self-care tools I will use. _(List at least three and use each
one for at least thirty minutes.)_

_____

_____

_____

Who can I call or text? _(List at least three people and
make sure some are available 24/7.)_

_____

_____

_____

How will I know I don't need to use this safety plan
anymore?

_____

_____

_____

our mental illness, and it's awful. I know the alternative can be a bit scary because it's unfamiliar but, trust me, we already know what our other option is, and this one is much better.

I admitted I needed help and in doing so, no longer had to hold the walls of my life together. Instead of being spread out in a big X on the ground trying to keep things from collapsing, I was able to stand tall. I was surrounded by the rubble of the walls that held me captive for many years but finally admitted, "This is my mess, and I am not strong enough to fix it on my own, please help me." I found that acknowledging weakness and being vulnerable helped me feel stronger than I had ever felt, while also filling me with fear. Along with that fear, though, I felt peace knowing that I was no longer fighting alone. I knew that if needed, I had friends I could call, whether it be to get through eating a meal or to talk me out of going for a run and risking more medical complications. When I looked in the mirror and insecurities tried to grip me and pull me back into negative behaviors, a new voice also spoke up and shared love for me, just as I was. Sharing where I was honestly at emotionally and the struggle with my eating disorder became easier over time. I didn't feel the need to pretend anymore. I just wanted to be real and honest, and in that act began to find healing.

There will be times during your path to self-improvement when you want to give up because it feels too hard and you're tired of fighting, but stick with it. Remember all the reasons you started on this path in the first place, and don't lose hope. Through hard work and persistence, you will learn who you truly are and who deserves the opportunity and privilege of being in your life.

Don't listen to naysayers; instead listen to this: you always have the power to change your life. You can push past any urges or struggles and become the best version of yourself. Yes, it will be hard, and feel like you are caught in an internal battle, but the fight will be worth it. You're worth it.

Epilogue

I want to make sure this part is clear: I am no better than you. I don't have all the answers, and I make mistakes too. What I do know is that with the right help it can and will get better, and that's the message I hope you heard throughout this book.

I know that all of the choices, reasons, and options can feel overwhelming, but breathe and take that first step. You will never regret reaching out for help when you need it. I know I haven't, and seeing a therapist to talk things through and gain some perspective will always be part of my life. It's helped me recognize parts of myself that I love and want to cultivate, and others I am ashamed of and want to snuff out. Allow the trained professionals in your area the chance to help you change. All you may feel, or whatever you've been through, isn't too much. You are important, and you deserve to feel better.

This book is yours to use however you see fit, whether that's as a road map to your own recovery, or even as a gift for someone who you know is suffering. Whatever you do with it, even if you let it collect dust on your shelf, just promise me that you won't stop talking about mental health. Talk about mental health with those you care about most, or find a professional you can vent to about what you are going through. Whatever you do, just keep talking, because it's only in the silence that the stigma surrounding mental illness can exist. Let's work together to shed light on the truth and keep the positive conversation about mental health going. I know I will.

appendix a:
glossary

Anxiety: The most common mental illness, and part of our fight-or-flight response. Excessive nervousness, unease, or worry about current or imagined situations. Anxiety can have a trigger, but often feels like it comes out of nowhere.

Art and music therapy: Types of therapy that rely on the patient's free expression of issues or concerns through the medium of art or music. It is imperative that this only be completed with a trained and licensed professional. May be utilized at any age, and practiced in a group or in individual sessions. Art and music therapy can help us express what we are going through when words are not easy to come up with. It can help us feel less isolated and give us a healthy outlet for what we may be going through.

Borderline personality disorder (BPD): The most misunderstood mental illness, BPD is a pervasive (not episodic) disorder characterized by feelings of abandonment, impulsivity, and struggles with interpersonal relationships. It can leave us feeling very vulnerable to any emotional attack, and in turn cause us to lash out at those we care about.

Cognitive behavioral therapy (CBT): Directive and short term, CBT focuses on our thoughts and how they decide our actions and feelings. Figuring out where our distorted thoughts come from, and recognizing that they are in fact faulty, is the goal. It is the most statistically effective form of treatment available.

Depression: Having a depressed mood, lack of interest in things we used to like, and even struggling to concentrate or get out of bed. Depression can feel different from person to person, but it comes and goes, affecting our ability to function in life.

Dialectical behavior therapy (DBT): While building off of what cognitive behavioral therapy does, DBT also works on helping us better regulate our emotions so we can acknowledge them and manage them, rather than feel they are running the show. DBT was created as a way to better treat those with borderline personality disorder.

Eating disorder (ED): An obsession with food; how to get it, not eat it, control it, exercise it off, etc. Also, using food as a way to cope with an overwhelming feeling. An ED can manifest as undereating, overeating, or doing things to make up for what we ate.

Exposure therapy: Best for phobias and fear-based issues, this style works by creating our fear hierarchy, building up our relaxation techniques, and slowly exposing us to the feared thing. After a while, we realize it's not that scary, and our fear goes away. This is short term and usually doesn't have to be revisited.

Eye movement desensitization reprocessing (EMDR): Used primarily for those who have been through a trauma or other distressing event. This type of therapy is still being researched and understood. It is believed that by initiating eye movements, we are giving our brain the chance it needs to process the upsetting event. Focusing on the trauma while your eyes move from left to right is supposed to take away the intense emotions associated with the experience.

Family therapy: Similar to group therapy, family therapy is an excellent addition to individual treatment. The focus of this style is to help a family work better together so the whole system is supported. Each person is challenged to see their role in the family's dysfunction; members work together to change. This is the second most effective treatment available.

Group therapy: Great as a supplement to individual therapy, group therapy can help us learn from other people's experiences, feel less isolated, and practice tools we are learning in our one-on-one therapy sessions. Groups can focus on a variety of issues, and utilize many types of therapy.

Licensed clinical social worker (LCSW): This professional has a master's degree in clinical social work. Social workers have been around the longest, and their focus is on helping you as an individual better manage your environment. This means helping you get a job or making sure you have all the government services you need to thrive. It's because of their focus that many LCSWs work in agencies and hospitals.

Licensed educational psychologist (LEP): An LEP has a master's degree or higher, and has spent at least three years within the school system. Most LEPs were school counselors before finishing their graduate programs and taking their licensing exams. The scope of their practice rests entirely within the educational system. They can offer testing and assessment for learning disabilities, as well as diagnose any mental illness that may affect our ability to learn. Overall, they ensure that any individual needs we may have at school are met and fully understood.

Licensed marriage and family therapist (LMFT): A therapist who has their master's in clinical psychology. Although the differences between the three main types of therapists aren't that significant, the focus of an LMFT is on relationships and helping you better manage any relationship causing you distress.

Licensed professional clinical counselor (LPCC): The newest addition to the therapy field, an LPCC has a master's degree in clinical counseling. Their focus is on helping you best manage a crisis, overcome addiction, and work through any issues you feel have been holding you back. Overall, they tend to be the broadest type of therapist in my listing. They do not focus exclusively on one aspect of someone's situation (e.g., relationships or environment); instead, they work from a more general perspective.

Mental health: How we are doing both psychologically and emotionally. We all have mental health that needs to be tended to daily.

Mental illness: Mental health that has been compromised to the point that it hinders our ability to function in daily life.

Psychiatric nurse (PMH-APRN): A registered nurse who went on to get a master's degree or doctorate in psychology. Depending on their level of education they can offer therapy, assessments, and in many states even write prescriptions. They bring both the medical and psychological models of treatment to their patients. Make sure you ask what they are able to help you with, since different states and licensure expand or limit what they can offer you.

Psychiatrist: A medical doctor who will help you get proper medication for your mental health issues. Usually they will only see you for fifteen to twenty minutes.

Psychoanalysis: Long-term treatment based on the theory that all humans are driven by their instincts and biological drives, and which focuses on looking into how our unconscious mind affects us each day. I only mentioned it to give you an idea of where therapy began. This isn't practiced often and can take a very long time. I personally would not recommend this treatment.

Psychologist: A therapist with a doctorate in psychology. They can have either a PhD or PsyD depending on whether they focused on research or seeing patients one on one. They may also offer various tests and assessments you might find helpful.

Talk therapy (psychotherapy): The most well-rounded approach, talk therapy is based on the premise that we can benefit from talking about our issues with a professional. Since *talk therapy* is an umbrella term, it allows a therapist to pick and choose from a variety of therapeutic styles. The goal is to help you better manage any issue or disorder causing you distress.

appendix b:
helpful resources and reminders

When Making Your First Appointment, Remember to . . .

1. leave your name and age.

2. include what's going on and how long you've been dealing with it.

3. ask about payment options and cost.

4. mention days and times that work with your schedule.

How to Know If They Are Right for You

1. You feel pretty comfortable talking to them.

2. You like the way their office feels.

3. You look forward to therapy, even though it's hard work.

Signs You Are Seeing a Bad Therapist

1. They don't remember important things you have told them.

2. They talk about themselves and their issues for most of your session.

3. They downplay your struggles or concerns, and you feel you have to prove how badly you are doing.

4. They don't have healthy boundaries and allow you to contact them 24/7.

5. There is no end of therapy in sight. They don't have any goals or a treatment plan they are following to ensure you are moving in the right direction.

6. They tell you what to do instead of listening to your thoughts and beliefs about your issue.

7. They cancel all the time and you don't feel like a priority.

Signs You Are Seeing a Good Therapist

1. You feel they are on your side rooting for you.

2. They clearly communicate what they are doing and listen to your thoughts as well.

3. They challenge you to do more, try harder, and push past what you used to think you could accomplish.

4. They give you feedback that describes how you are feeling. They validate your experience.

5. They check in on your progress and make sure you feel you are moving toward your goals at a good pace.

Seven Helpful Communication Skills to Use
in Your Relationships

1. Stick to the Facts: When trying to make a point, stick to the facts instead of letting judgment or emotions get in the way. This also ensures we are taken seriously.

2. Be Empathic: Put yourself in the other person's shoes for a bit. Can you see things from their point of view? This doesn't mean you agree with them, just that you can see why they interpreted the scenario the way they did.

3. Take Turns: In order to resolve any conflict or get someone else to listen to us we need to take turns talking. In my practice I use a yellow piece of paper called "the floor" to give each person the time they need to talk. Everyone listening has to repeat back what they heard, then the next person can go. This gives each participant uninterrupted time to share their side and be heard.

4. Be an Equal: Talking down to someone else never helps a conversation or a relationship. Make sure you are hearing their side, connecting over the things you have in common, and working together to resolve any conflict. No one is ever a hundred percent right in a situation, so be open to listening to their perspective.

5. Make It Personal: Using "I" statements can help keep us from blaming someone else for how we feel, and when used properly, they can assist us in sharing our feelings

or view of things without opinion or judgment. Notice how often you say, "You make me . . . ," "I feel that you . . . ," or "I like that you . . ." These statements are not necessarily harmful every time they are used, but they can lead us into a more judgmental or blaming conversation.

6. Ask Questions: Asking questions can help keep us from making assumptions and getting upset when we don't need to. Make sure you ask appropriate questions to ensure you fully understand the situation before jumping to conclusions.

7. Be Open to Compromise: It would be nice to live in a world where we all wanted the same things at the same time, but save yourself the stress and recognize it never happens like that. Instead, people have different plans, expectations, and desires. Working together so we each get some of what we want is what keeps relationships going, and why compromising is part of every happy and healthy partnership.

Five Most Common Communication Mistakes

1. Keeping Score: This term refers to keeping track of all you or your partner have or have not done in your relationship. For example, saying you have cleaned the house more times than them, and then you use the score you have kept against them to make them feel bad or to get them to clean the house. This is toxic to any partnership because it attaches strings to anything we should be doing out of love and joy.

2. Passive Aggression: Doing small things to make another's life difficult when we don't have the tools or knowledge to express how we are feeling. Journaling or taking notes to better understand what we may be going through can help us stop acting in this way. Also, working to communicate with those around us in a more direct and caring fashion can stop this failure-to-communicate-directly blunder from happening.

3. Communication Filters: We all act from our own life filters. Due to our past experiences we may assume that situations will turn out a certain way without having any current evidence to support our belief. These assumptions can create conflict and upset where none need have existed. Understanding what our filters are and asking clarifying questions are the best ways to overcome this.

4. Never Say Never: These are phrases like "You always do that!" or "You never help me clean the house!" Speaking in extremes and absolutes separates us from our partner and blames them for upsets. Being mindful of how often we use words like always, never, can't, hate, wouldn't, and couldn't is the best way to break this bad habit.

5. Fighting Doesn't Mean Breakup: We will all get into fights with those we care about. Having a disagreement shouldn't mean that we will break up or get divorced, and allowing that belief into a relationship strips it of trust and comfort. What solidifies our connection to others is the ability to disagree and be upset, but to choose the relationship over the fight. Give yourself the opportunity to let people in, allow them to get to know you, and lovingly deal with any argument.

Five Red Flags That You Need More Help

1. We find the time in therapy goes by too quickly and we don't feel we can talk about all we need to. We are always left wanting more time and feeling we aren't making any progress.

2. Urges to go back to using an unhealthy coping skill are getting stronger.

3. We aren't able to talk about any of the things we truly need to because it's just too difficult.

4. We struggle to tell our therapist the truth. This could be lying and saying we are doing well so they don't recommend more care, or pretending to be worse than we are in order to stay in therapy. Whatever the case, not being able to be honest with our therapist or other treatment team members shows us that we need to make some changes to our level of care.

5. Not being able to function in daily life. If we can't take care of our basic needs (e.g., showering, feeding ourselves, getting to work or school), then we need more support.

The Different Levels of Care Available

Outpatient Treatment: This is the lowest level of care, and where most people start when they seek help. We go in for our sessions each week and then go about our daily life. We are able to keep up with most of our responsibilities; we just need some support and guidance each week. This is also easy for people to integrate because it's only an hour or two a week and can fit into almost any schedule.

Intensive Outpatient Programs (IOPs): If we have tried increasing our outpatient sessions and we still feel that we are getting worse, there are IOPs. These are usually specific to the issue or diagnosis we are working on and can still be done while working or going to school. These programs usually run for ten to twenty hours over a span of three to five days a week. They usually include one-on-one therapy, group therapy, and sessions with a psychiatrist.

Partial Hospitalization Programs (PHPs): These are the next step up in treatment and are usually offered at the same clinic as intensive outpatient programs. They are very much the same as IOPs, but much more intensive and time consuming. At this stage you will need to take a leave from school or work in order to attend the program. These programs are the highest level of care we can receive and still live in our own home; they run all day, five to seven days a week. Any of these treatment levels can be used as step-down options while coming out of a more intensive treatment program.

Inpatient/Residential Treatment: If spending most of our days in treatment isn't helping us improve, this is the next step up, and it requires that we live at a treatment facility. All your therapeutic needs are met with group and individual sessions, as well as any other medical checkups you may require. Treatment at this level means we are not a danger to ourselves or anyone else, yet are not able to make positive choices for our recovery on our own, and require round-the-clock support.

Hospitalization: We may consider hospitalization if we worry that we could harm ourselves or someone we love. Being in a locked facility ensures that no one gets hurt and we get the professional help we need. Hospitalization is also helpful if we struggle to commit to treatment or have tried to leave a clinic in the past, because most hospitals have locked programs where you have to check in for a certain amount of time and are not allowed to leave. It's also helpful if our illness is harmful to our physical health, as it gives us full access to medical attention and psychological help at the same time.

How to Prevent Relapse

Identify Your Triggers: Start noticing what sets you off and makes you want to go back to your unhealthy coping skills. It can even help to go back to when you first experienced these symptoms, or the first time you started acting out. We have to know what upsets us in order to be able to better manage it.

Identify Your Relapse Symptoms: What signs or symptoms do you experience prior to a relapse? These could be changes in sleep or appetite, or maybe just being more negative about ourselves and those around us. Whatever it is, take note and start paying attention to how you feel. Recognizing these symptoms early on can give us time to implement helpful tools.

Increase Self-Care: Taking care of our own needs first gives us more patience and energy, which makes it easier to fight off any urges to relapse. We should be making time for these things each day. They can be simple activities like going for a walk, showering, or eating well. Make time to take care of yourself so that when those unhealthy urges crop back up, you are more than able to manage them.

Create a Safety Plan: This can be done with a therapist or on your own. It should be something you create when you are feeling good and doing well. It needs to include a prompt for you to write down the symptoms you are experiencing and a list of self-care items you will utilize when you are struggling, as well as how long you need to do them. It should also have a list of supportive people you can reach out to in the moment and a prompt asking you how you will know you don't need to do these helpful things anymore. This framework gives us a plan for those times we may want to give in to our impulses and relapse.

Reach Out for Help: This is also part of many of the other tools offered, but it's important to know you can reach out. You deserve to get support and help when you need it most, so don't wait! The sooner we start talking about how we feel and what's going on, the less likely it is to turn into a relapse.

notes

Chapter 1. What Is Mental Health?
What You Should Know and Where to Start

1. National Institute of Mental Health, "Any Mental Illness (AMI) Among Adults," https://www.nimh.nih.gov/health/statistics/mental-illness .shtml.

2. Ibid.

3. National Institute of Mental Health, "Anxiety Disorders," March 2016, https://www.nimh.nih.gov/health/topics/anxiety-disorders/index.shtml.

4. Anxiety and Depression Association of America, "Facts & Statistics," August 2016, https://adaa.org/about-adaa/press-room/facts-statistic.

Chapter 3. How Do I Know If I Need Help?
Warning Signs and What to Look For

1. National Alliance on Mental Illness, "Mental Health by the Numbers," October 2016, https://www.nami.org/learn-more/mental-health-by-the -numbers.

2. RIKEN, "Why Do Babies Calm Down When They Are Carried?," April 19, 2013, http://www.riken.jp/en/pr/press/2013/20130419_2/.

3. Mental Health America, "The State of Mental Health in America," 2017, http://www.mentalhealthamerica.net/issues/state-mental-health -america.

Chapter 4. Mental Health Professionals Decoded:
Who Does What?

1. American Psychiatric Nurses Association, *Psychiatric-Mental Health Nurses,* May 2014, https://www.apna.org/i4a/pages/index.cfm?pageid =3292#3.

2. University of Southern California, "9 Most Influential Women in the History of Social Work," March 13, 2014, https://msw.usc.edu/mswusc -blog/9-most-influential-women-in-the-history-of-social-work/.

3. California Board of Behavioral Sciences, "Licensed Professional Clinical Counselor Information," 2016, http://www.bbs.ca.gov/applicants/ lpcc.html.

Chapter 5. What Is Best for Me?
Finding the Right Kind of Therapy

1. Gerry Grossman Seminars, *Counseling Theory in a Flash,* March 2009, https://gerrygrossman.com/mall/products.php?cat=9&SKU =GGS0008.

2. Matthew McKay, Jeffrey C. Wood, and Jeffrey Brantley, *The Dialectical Behavior Therapy Skills Workbook* (Oakland, CA: New Harbinger, 2007).

3. American Psychological Association, "Procedures and Guidelines for Group Therapy," April 2011, http://www.apadivisions.org/division-49 /publications/newsletter/group-psychologist/2011/04/group-procedures .aspx.

4. INSERM Collective Expertise Centre, "Psychotherapy: Three Approaches Evaluated," 2000, https://www.ncbi.nlm.nih.gov/books/ NBK7123/.

5. American Psychological Association, "What Is Exposure Therapy?," February 2017, http://www.apa.org/ptsd-guideline/patients-and-families/ exposure-therapy.aspx.

6. EMDR Institute, "Efficacy of EMDR," 2013, http://www.emdr.com/efficacy/.

7. American Music Therapy Association, "What Is Music Therapy?," 2015, https://www.musictherapy.org/about/musictherapy/.

8. American Art Therapy Association, "What Is Art Therapy?," 2013, https://arttherapy.org/about-art-therapy/.

Chapter 7. Is My Therapist a Good Fit?
Feeling the "Click" in a Therapeutic Relationship

1. Simply Psychology, *John Bowlby's Attachment Theory*, 2007, https://www.simplypsychology.org/attachment.html.

2. Bretherton, *The Origins of Attachment Theory: John Bowlby and Mary Ainsworth*, 1992, http://cmapspublic2.ihmc.us/rid=1LQX400NM-RBVKH9-1KL6/the%20origins%20of%20attachment%20theory%20john%20bowlby%20and_mary_ainsworth.pdf.

Chapter 8. What Are Toxic Relationships?
Warning Signs and Ways to Get Out of Them

1. Lenore Walkcr, *The Battered Woman* (New York: Harper and Row, 1979).

Chapter 9. Communication:
The Key to a Happy, Healthy Life!

1. Howard J. Markman, Scott M. Stanley, and Susan L. Blumberg, *Fighting for Your Marriage* (San Francisco: Jossey-Bass, 2001), 110–111.

index